How to Tutor Your Own Child

How to Tutor Your Own Child

Boost Grades and Inspire a Lifelong
Love of Learning—Without Paying
for a Professional Tutor

Marina Koestler Ruben

Foreword by Gerald Richards

TEN SPEED PRESS
Berkeley

Published in the United States by Ten Speed Press, an imprint of the
Crown Publishing Group, a division of Random House, Inc., New York.
www.crownpublishing.com
www.tenspeed.com

Ten Speed Press and the Ten Speed Press colophon are registered
trademarks of Random House, Inc.

Library of Congress Cataloging-in-Publication Data
Ruben, Marina Koestler.
  How to tutor your own child : boost grades and instill a lifelong love of
learning, without paying for a professional tutor / Marina Koestler Ruben.
       p. cm.
  Summary: "A top academic tutor gives parents the tools they need to inspire
after-school learning at home, without having to hire a pricey outside tutor"
—Provided by publisher.
  Includes bibliographical references and index.
  1. Tutors and tutoring. 2. Education—Parent participation. I. Title.
  LC41.R83 2011
  371.39'4—dc22

                              2010050451

ISBN 978-1-60774-027-8

Printed in the United States of America on recycled paper (20% PCW)

Design by Chloe Rawlins

Front cover photograph copyright © iStockphoto / Floortje

10 9 8 7 6 5 4 3 2

First Edition

Contents

Acknowledgments

Thanks, of course, to my own parent-tutors, Vicki and Bob Koestler. I'm sure my mother is responsible for my writing career, given that she still reviews (and significantly improves) everything I write. Likewise, I think my father inspired my brother's love of computers and my interest in logic problems and in French (which he taught me while brushing my baby teeth). Thanks to Dan Koestler for his technological expertise (for which he will be compensated indefinitely with homemade ice cream) and his knowledge about the transience of school papers.

Special thanks to Laurie Abkemeier, at DeFiore and Company, who provided me with months of helpful advice before she even saw the proposal for this book and made it possible, within the span of a year, for two Rubens to provide publishers with books that have sections about mnemonic devices. And many thanks to everyone at Ten Speed Press, especially Lisa Westmoreland who edited this book.

Thanks, too, to Katie McLane, the owner of Potomac Tutors, who rekindled my enthusiasm for education and learning when I worked for her. And to Janna Taylor, who hired me at Potomac Tutors and now runs her own company, Mind Full Tutors.

So many others provided helpful feedback for this book, including Sarah Arikian; Nikki Bravo; Anne Charny; Anthony Dellureficio; Mike Fishback; Raina Fishbane; Gerard Hagen; Trudi Hagen; Nuit Hansgen; Elizabeth Ide; Ellen Kittredge; Diana Lazarus; Angela and Elaine Magnan; Tom Mansell; Ryoko Matsumoto; Jane Miller; Kenneth Quittman; Michelle Schneck; Scot Slaby; Rebecca Wallace-Segall; and Sara White (and her coworkers, students, family, and friends). Thanks to Alyson, Matt, Mimi, Rhea, and Taylor for your feedback and suggestions.

Thanks, of course, to my husband, Adam Ruben, who sacrificed large portions of a beach vacation to read drafts of this book. He recently published his own book ostensibly about helping students, *Surviving Your Stupid, Stupid Decision to Go to Grad School*. His book is antieducation and mine is proeducation; I'm hoping the two books don't cosmically cancel each other out.

Foreword

Parents, let me tell you two things. First, your children think you're amazing. Seriously. You may not think so and they may not say so (at least until they turn twenty-five or thirty) but they do. Second, you were your child's best teacher. You taught them right from wrong and how to tie their shoes. I say *were* because around first grade you were replaced. Replaced by Ms. Dunbar in the first grade or Mr. Silver the hip English teacher—and that's okay. It provides you with the opportunity to take on another role in your child's education, that of tutor. Your child listens and pays attention to everything you say or do. So it's only natural that your child learn about Ptolemy, practice quadratic equations, and recite Shakespeare's sonnets with you. Marina Koestler Ruben wrote this book to show you how.

At our 826 tutoring centers, we have over five thousand volunteers who work with our students every day. They help students with math, reading, and writing. For various reasons, many of our students' parents don't have the time or the capacity to help their children. Our volunteer tutors provide these students with a caring adult willing to spend a couple of hours of their time working with a young person on their homework. It means the world to our students to have someone spend that much time where the spotlight is on them, what they are working on, and how they can be helped. We provide training to our volunteers because tutoring can be scary. Having that young face look at you hoping you have all the answers can be an intimidating experience. We work to make tutoring fun and simple so that the tutor and the student both have the best experience possible.

I remember my first tutor. I was (and kind of still am) horrible at math. I scored a 275 on the math portion of my SATs. 275. I wasn't going to get into a good college—in fact, I worried I might not even get into college. My school assigned me a professional math tutor, a stodgy, socially awkward man—who smelled. But he was a great tutor. He was knowledgeable, very tough, and very patient. After two months of tutoring, I scored a 400. Not perfect, but a score that got me into a great college. I know the difference tutoring can make in a life.

This book empowers you to become the tutor, that additional teacher your child may need to achieve educational success. It provides you with positive reinforcement to let you know that you don't have to be a Rhodes Scholar to help your child prepare for a chemistry test. You just need the time and the desire. I know you have both. This book provides you with the tips and tools you'll need to make tutoring your child an enjoyable experience for you both. Learning doesn't have to be confined to school. It can take place in the kitchen, the dining room, or the backyard.

A PhD is not required to help your child learn. There's no mystery or secret sauce. Your child already thinks you're amazing, and being your child's tutor is just another sign of how great you are. Marina is giving you her secrets and her years of experience. She has given you tips and demystified the process. You have decided to become not just a parent but also that caring adult all children need. Have fun!

Gerald Richards
CEO
826 National

826 National is a network of nonprofit organizations cofounded by Dave Eggers and dedicated to helping students, ages six to eighteen, with expository and creative writing, and to helping teachers inspire their students to write. 826 chapters are located in San Francisco, Los Angeles, New York, Chicago, Ann Arbor, Seattle, Boston, and Washington, DC. Our mission is based on the understanding that great leaps in learning can happen with one-on-one attention, and that strong writing skills are fundamental to future success.

Introduction:
The Best Tutors I
Never Knew I Had

The first time I tutored, I had déjà vu. I was a high school student, and Suji, the girl sitting next to me, was my friend's younger sister, so I had seen her dozens of times before this algebra session. But our previous interactions didn't account for my feeling that I had been here before. Perhaps déjà vu is not quite the right phrase, because I didn't think I had been in *my* seat before, as Suji's tutor. Rather, I felt like I'd been in *hers*, as a tutee.

But why did I feel this way? I was stumped. After all, my brother and I regularly did our homework tutorless, often at our family's dining table. Overall, we were good students, but we certainly had deficiencies: I regularly procrastinated, and it appeared Dan used his backpack to collect debris from loose-leaf-paper war zones. At times, we had failed quizzes and been stumped by difficult concepts. Yet I don't think our parents ever suggested tutoring. Until I became a tutor myself, I'm not sure they knew that the service existed for anyone besides royalty and child stars.

Sitting there next to Suji, thinking about all those afternoons of homework, I realized that I was mistaken. Dan and I *had* had people who sat us down to sort when our folders overflowed, who guided us in outlining papers when deadlines loomed, who read over our essays, quizzed us on spelling and vocabulary, pointed us toward noteworthy newspaper articles, and asked us to calculate cost per ounce in the grocery store. We had not grown up tutorless. Rather, we had taken our tutors for granted. We had been sitting in Suji's seat—had *lived* in Suji's seat—every day as our mentors motivated, educated, and laughed with us. We had been lucky enough to share two de facto tutors: our parents.

Today, as an educator, I see that it is increasingly common for parents to delegate to outside tutors the job of providing their children with academic support. While I risk putting myself out of a job by saying this, I firmly believe that professional tutors should not replace (only *supplement*, if necessary) the kind of positive, one-on-one, scholarly interaction that parents and students should share on a daily basis.

How to Tutor Your Own Child builds on the idea that you *can* and *should* be academically engaged with your own child on a regular basis. As a professional tutor, I'd like to use the knowledge gleaned from my tutoring experience with hundreds of students to show you how.

Throughout this book, I will share with you my firm belief that the best tutor a child can have is his or her own parent. Parent-tutors provide holistic, low-pressure academic support, engagement, and enrichment for their children. They are supportive and inspirational, and they believe in the importance of creating an intellectually stimulating environment in the home. Day in and day out, they can see their children learn and develop, and as a student's desire and capacity for knowledge grow, the parent-child relationship grows as well.

Perhaps you want to be a parent-tutor but don't know where to start. Or maybe you are one already and want to hone your skills. You may be providing stellar one-on-one support and just want to compare your tutoring techniques to those used by professionals. In any case, if you want to tutor a child, this book is for you.

While discussing this book in the faculty room at Sidwell Friends School, where I work, I mentioned the concept of the tutoring lifestyle to a teacher who has two young children. She broke into maniacal laughter. When she stopped (eventually) to breathe, she told me she had pictured waking up her kids to show them math flash cards. She couldn't imagine a lifestyle of constant tutoring. "Good luck," I believe she said.

I realized I needed to be sure readers, too, didn't assume that the "tutoring lifestyle" requires unceasing, didactic, and pedantic fact drills. Adopting a tutoring lifestyle and choosing to work with your own child does not mean that you must strain to instruct your child at every waking moment, nor that you must interrupt your child's slumber to shine a flashlight on a mountain of flashcards. Rather, it means that you will, gradually, retrain yourself to perceive your child's environment as an educator would; to consider what your child does and does not understand about the world around her; and to grab opportunities to augment what happens at school, with a special appreciation for the subjects about which your child naturally expresses interest. It means choosing to take an active part in engaging your child's intellect and finding enjoyable, positive ways to do so. By tutoring, you build a relationship with your child. If, at any point, the strain it places on your relationship or on the family dynamic outweighs the positives, something is wrong, and you should stop. Tutoring is not torture—it's shared learning.

If critics tell you, "Parents shouldn't tutor," explain that "tutoring" is the process of turning children into lifelong learners and is, therefore, a form of high-quality parenting. Those same critics wouldn't claim, "Parents shouldn't parent," would they?

Even if you have hired or plan to hire an outside tutor, keep in mind that your child will not always have the tutor there. More days than not, *you* will be your child's primary educator and role model, meaning that you should still prepare yourself to emulate the techniques of a professional tutor.

As one of my friends said, "No one will ever love your child more than you do, so educate yourself about your children's needs." Learn how they learn. It's your role and—if you're reading this—one you already value, which means you're on the right path.

Over the past ten years of tutoring, I have interacted with hundreds of students and parents. My recommendations come from working with children of all ages and backgrounds, from pre-K through twelfth grade, from "remedial" to "enhancement," from recently resettled refugees who couldn't speak a word of English to privileged students in some of the wealthiest communities in America. I've tried to cull from these experiences the information that has applied most universally and been of greatest help to parents and students.

Even so, you might find some of this book's advice absurd. You might laugh aloud and say, "My child would never sit still for that!" And you're probably right.

Not all the advice in this book will work for every student, nor should it. Some recommendations are meant for younger children, while others are meant for middle or high school students. Don't feel you need to embrace every technique in this book—instead, make use of the bits and pieces that strike you as worth a try. The tools described in this book comprise the abundance of options a professional tutor has on hand; the tutor considers which are appropriate for any given student. You, too, should equip yourself and then pick and choose to fit the student and the moment.

When you encounter ideas that *won't* work for your child, keep reading. You'll likely come across ideas or troubleshooting tricks that *will* work. Bottom line: You know your children better than I do. When it comes to tutoring, that's the point.

CHAPTER 1

Starting Out:
Why Tutor?

Princeton Review, Huntington Learning Center, Sylvan Learning Center, Kaplan Tutoring, SCORE—America is awash in tutoring companies. It's a $4 billion industry, and it seems as if every helicopter parent is buying in. If only there were a resource closer to home that was easy, free, and able to provide the same quality of service that students receive with an outside tutor. But there is: *you*.

Tutoring is the academic word for *parenting*. Just as a parent guides his or her child in developing practical life skills, a tutor helps a student learn how to learn academically and intellectually. As a parent, there's no reason you can't participate in the tutoring process. Who better than parents to help their children learn to walk or say their first words? Likewise, when it comes to scholastics, parents' care and contributions can be priceless.

HOW YOUR CHILD BENEFITS

When school instruction is insufficient to meet a child's needs or interests, parent-tutoring can fill the gap. Not only can it benefit children academically, helping to engender a lifelong passion for learning, but it also inspires them socially and emotionally by enhancing their powers of conversation and modeling empathetic listening. In the process, students gain a level of support and motivation that many parents might not realize they have the power to provide.

Whether you're a parent, a grandparent, or an older friend or family member, your presence as a role model may be more significant than you realize. A close friend told me the story of how, when her father was nineteen, he inadvertently became a role model for his twelve-year-old sister. The sister enjoyed reading Nancy Drew books, but one day she was poking around in her brother's room and found the book *Lord of the Flies*, which he had read for a college English class. Some older brothers might shoo a younger sister out of the room or tell her to stop going through their belongings. But this brother did something different: he not only offered to lend her the book, but he also told his sister that, if she read it, he would discuss it with her.

Now, this didn't seem like a big deal at the time, at least not to the older brother. His sister read the book, they discussed it, end of story. He forgot about it for good. But over forty years later, at a family gathering, the incident came up—as did its significance. As it turned out, her brother's offer to discuss *Lord of the Flies* was the first time anyone had ever given this girl the opportunity to engage on a sophisticated literary level. She found it so inspirational that she credited the experience with kindling her lifelong love of Hemingway, Fitzgerald, and Saroyan, and of literature as a whole.

That's the power of one moment—one small instance of reaching out. You have the opportunity to make the same choice. And to make it again and again, every day, allowing your child to benefit from thousands of such moments with you over the years. My friend's father didn't know that his book discussion would be the key to one of his sister's passions; likewise, you might not know for years—if ever—which of the many moments you spend with your child will provide lasting inspiration. But just as the hours you spend talking to your baby eventually lead to a child who can speak, the short-term and long-term benefits of one-on-one intellectual engagement will be similarly well worth your time. Your interaction does not have to be formal, nor does it have to be consistently "academic." All you really have to do is to find little ways to *show* and *share* your love of learning, and your child will do the rest.

HOW YOU BENEFIT

Sometimes when I tell people that I'm a professional tutor, they adopt a sympathetic look. "Do you think you'd want to get a job as an English teacher?" they ask, immediately trying to think of ways I could move up in the world.

There's an assumption, both within and outside the educational sector, that a hierarchy exists and that the lowest rung is populated by tutors and freshmen.

Don't tell the English teachers, but it turns out the perks of tutoring can be just as rewarding as those of teaching. For you, as a parent-tutor, here's what that means: As they say—or as they should say—what's good for the gosling is good for the goose and gander. In other words, tutoring benefits parents as well as students. Besides reviewing academic content, parents also learn more about their own children, their children's learning style, and how best to communicate—a skill handy when tutoring and when interacting with family, friends, and coworkers.

Most important, as a parent-tutor you have the satisfaction of knowing that you are investing in someone who will not be with you for just a semester or a year—you will have the joy of seeing the effects of your involvement over a lifetime.

SO WHAT IS TUTORING EXACTLY?

Tutoring means different things to different people, but, at its core, it's a combination of homework help, strengthening weaker skills, and enrichment. It may come in the form of a one-hour, deliberately scheduled session, or it may be sprinkled throughout your child's week in the form of general support and interaction. You probably tutor your child already—my goal is to get you to develop the techniques, resources, and communication necessary to make this time more productive.

As a parent-tutor, you have advantages that I as an outside tutor do not. You have access to your child all the time. You can monitor whether he is following through, expose him to educational home elements, set rules and boundaries, and follow his progress long term. An outside tutor is a relatively poor substitute for an involved parent-tutor and should only be used as needed for specialty tutoring, when a parent is not available, or when an interpersonal issue makes the parent-child relationship strained. The parent-tutor is the generalist who supports the child regularly.

Your child will learn by exposure. Your goal is to keep him impassioned and motivated. Remember that tutoring is about more than just subject matter. "When students seek tutoring," says Janna Taylor, the owner of New York's Mind Full Tutors, "while on the surface it may appear that they just want to know how to learn a certain concept (e.g., use the Pythagorean theorem or memorize the steps of cellular respiration), the truth is that what they really want is to feel secure and supported. Because parents often feel an instinctual need to provide security and support for their children anyway, tutoring can be another wonderful opportunity for them to extend this element of parenting."[1]

Tutoring ≠ Teaching

Sometimes parents balk at the idea of one-on-one work with their own child. Amid the chorus of fears, common concerns emerge.

YOU: But I don't have a teaching degree.

YOU: But isn't this the teacher's job?

YOU: But I don't know anything about ancient Babylonia!

Pull yourself together. Here's a reality check that doubles as a math refresher: Tutoring ≠ Teaching.

Please note that I did not say "Tutoring > Teaching." Nor did I say "Tutoring < Teaching."* There is no hierarchy. And, while it's true that

---

* Remember that we say ">" as "greater than" and "<" as "less than." See the section on visual mnemonics (page 87) for a trick to help remember this.

the skills involved in teaching and tutoring overlap, they differ enough that you are certainly equipped to be your child's tutor.

Traditionally, teachers introduce a group of students to a topic. Teachers select curricula, decide how best to communicate it to their classes, and then reinforce the material with assignments, discussions, and assessments. Let's say your child's class is learning about Greek mythology. The teacher hands out the family tree of the Titans' next of kin, decides which students make the three-dimensional model of the Oracle at Delphi and which make Zeus and Hera sock puppets, and tells your child whether or not he will be responsible for residents of the Underworld for the test.*

Once an individual student has been exposed to a topic at school, the tutor reviews it at home. The tutor talks through that mythological family tree, making sure a child understands the way its branches indicate relationships. The tutor helps the student decide whether to use sugar cubes or popsicle sticks for the Oracle, discussing structural and aesthetic factors. In hunting for appropriate socks, the tutor prompts a child to describe what qualities Zeus and Hera socks would ideally have (woolly and rip-proof? green with jealousy?), thereby subtly encouraging students to review characteristics of the Greek gods.

---

* If your child is really studying Greek mythology, check out Rick Riordan's *Percy Jackson & the Olympians* series. The first book is *The Lightning Thief* (Hyperion, 2010). It's like Harry Potter, but kids get enthused about mythology while they read.

Tutors make sure that individual students learn. More than that, they make sure that students know *how* to learn. They motivate, guide, and mentor. Think of yourself as a personal learning coordinator.

The Perils of Knowing Too Little or Too Much

YOU: But I still have a problem. I don't know anything about Greek mythology or ancient Babylonia or even modern Babylonia!

Here's this book's first big secret. It helps to have a basic understanding of a subject in order to help a student, but it is *not necessary*. This is what a good tutor does in your situation:

Option 1: Learn as you go. If you don't have time to read up on your own, have your child *teach you*. Follow along.

Option 2: Research as needed. You'll model good research skills for your child.

Option 3: Truly stumped? Don't make something up—tell your child to ask the teacher. This helps him remember that the teacher is always there as a resource.

YOU: I have a different problem. I know *too much* about ancient Babylonia! My child tunes me out when I try to talk about King Nebuchadnezzar's conquest in 587 BCE.

Often, it can be as complicated for parents who are *over*educated in a subject to tutor as it is for parents who feel *under*educated. When you've spent eight years getting a PhD in meteorology, you might have trouble talking your child through a simple discussion of cirrus, cumulus, and stratus clouds without going into detail about the pre-

---

TUTOR TOOLBOX

If a child has questions about school assignments, her first resource should still be the teacher.

---

cise altitude of each cloud layer, creating distinctions using specialized vocabulary (*Cumulus castellanus* versus *Cumulus congestus*), and falling into a college-level lecture. (Or, more likely, you might rush through the concepts in your child's arithmetic homework because you are already a master of long division.) Remember, part of tutoring is being cognizant of your child's level of understanding and building interest *at that level.* When you know too much, here's what to do:

- Cover the basics first. And ask enough questions to be sure your child understands the material.

- Use your knowledge to provide story-like details. *Cumulus castellanus* may be less interesting when you talk in terms of vertical and lateral cloud movement but can become a lot more interesting when you explain that *castellanus* has to do with *castles* and that the clouds look like castle turrets in the sky.

- Engage your child with an interactive visual aid. I can imagine a cloud that has turrets, but if I have to draw one and compare it to a photograph or point to one in the sky, I'm going to remember it much more easily.

- If you want to provide your child with advanced knowledge of a subject and feel his attention straying, save some of that extra information for a time when it can be shared more organically, in a less academic context. (Point out clouds when you're out for a walk, for example.)

Plan Your Own Obsolescence

No, this is not a section on writing one's will. You are planning to do yourself in, but not in the traditional sense. *Your goal as a tutor is to make yourself obsolete.* To transfer ownership of the learning process to your child so that, ultimately, she is an expert at recognizing how she learns and then can use the most applicable skills to succeed academically, intellectually, and professionally.

Try, over time, to transition from a directive to a nondirective tutoring style. In directive tutoring, the tutor has the dominant role. The tutor is making the decisions, leading the discussion, and doing *for* more than doing *with*.

In nondirective tutoring, you are *guiding* more than ruling. You are asking your child what she needs to do, not telling her. (If you or your child feels you are taking over your time together, you are probably erring on the side of helping too much.)

Raina Fishbane, the math resource teacher at Sidwell Friends School's Lower School, puts it simply when addressing parents who want to help their children solve math problems: "Don't hold the pencil." In other words, if you want to ensure that your child is the one leading the process, you might want to (literally) take control out of your own hands. Let your child initiate his own work, respond to your child's questions with your own open-ended questions ("What do *you* think would be a way you could approach this?"), and—perhaps hardest of all—don't stop your child the moment you see him making a mistake. As Raina puts it, "You want your *child* ultimately to have the 'Aha!' moment."[2]

As needed, it may be appropriate to have a more directive approach with younger children, children who are being tutored in a nonnative language, or students who have pronounced learning disabilities.

Point your child toward the mindset of the self-powered learner. At the start of sessions, ask your child to tell you what her goals are for the day (ditto for the start of a unit, semester, or year). When you see your child contemplating homework, ask what she is aiming to accomplish. You don't need to do this all the time—just enough to reassure yourself that your child is developing the ability to think longer term and set realistic goals.

Adopt this same transitional mentality within smaller areas and assignments. Does your child recognize and remove distractions? Does your child understand whether she needs to create short-term deadlines to get motivated about long-term assignments? What types of errors does she need to look for in rough drafts of papers? When your child doesn't know something, can she independently spot that lack of knowledge and find a way to remedy it?

When it comes to finding a place to work, your child should recognize the need to sweep aside clutter and find a clean, clear workspace. If she is trying to find a clear table and requests (nicely) that other family members move their belongings, try to acquiesce—your child is becoming an empowered self-advocate.

Your job is to show your child the resources she might need and how they can be used. Then you transfer to your child the responsibility of using them. You will not be sitting there to pull out the Post-its when your child is president; she will have to recognize her own need for them and have the motivation to get them herself.

LOVE LEARNING, NOT THE IVY LEAGUE

Sometimes it seems like the whole K–12 educational endeavor is about one thing: getting into college. Maybe in a way it is. But that doesn't seem right. So I want to launch into the rest of this book with the following suggestion: when you work with your child, try, just try, to imagine that your child is *not* going to college. You may already do this. But if not, try to imagine that the reason you are talking, working, and sharing knowledge with your child is because your child will need to be an educated and insightful human being and to understand how the world works, what happens, and why.

This mindset not only models for your child the most grounded, most ethical stance, but it also focuses your tutoring sessions on the easily forgotten point of education: learning.

TUTOR TAKE-AWAY

- Tutoring is not the same as teaching, so don't worry about not having a degree.

- You need not know the material; even professional tutors often learn as they go or do research as needed.

- A recommended goal: Transition your tutoring style from the directive to the nondirective.

- Forget college!

CHAPTER 2

Getting Down To It:
The Basics

First, let's talk about where you're going to be working and what supplies you should have nearby. Take a cue from the Zen-inspired 1970 cookbook, *The Tassajara Bread Book*, which includes recipes for several types of "Something Missing Muffins."[1] Eggless? There's a muffin recipe for that. No baking power? There's a muffin recipe for that. In the same vein, do not let a less-than-perfect workspace or supply kit discourage you. Ultimately, all you need for tutoring are two bodies (and their associated minds): yours and your child's.

THE WORKSPACE

This is simple. You need a **large, flat surface**. The surface can be a desk. A dining table. A coffee table. You can even get down to ground level, perhaps the living room or bedroom floor. In some communities, they do use the actual ground, on which students draw with sticks. Abraham Lincoln is said to have lain on the floor of his family's cabin to work, reading by the light of the fire.

Whatever the workspace, it should be **clear and clean**. Physical clutter has a way of fostering mental clutter. Avoid having paper strewn about. Corral stray books and papers and stack them neatly to the side. Dust, sweep, or vacuum the space, whether underfoot or tabled.

You and your child can sit near each other on desk chairs. Dining chairs. Bar stools. You can crouch or kneel at a coffee table. Some students work best at a standing desk—you can buy a special standing desk or find a surface of the appropriate height in your home.

You and your child should have **equal access** to the surface of the workspace during tutoring sessions. For this reason, it's preferable to sit at neutral ground, such as a dining or kitchen table, rather than pulling up a chair next to your child's desk (unless it's particularly spacious). Most important is that, during tutoring sessions, both tutor and child should feel at ease in the space.

If you have the luxury of choice, pick a **quiet** environment, ideally in a room where your child focuses best. Some students like to work where others will see their progress. They like the validation of doing work in public view. For others, the level of noise and distraction that that incurs is untenable. They have to work in isolation.

While I do recommend having a reliable, clean, supply-stocked space to use as a base of homework operations, research has shown the benefits of studying in varied locations. A student can set up shop at his desk, leaving the homework notebook and major supplies there, then rotate each afternoon to a new location with, for example, the day's list of vocabulary words or a history textbook. Contrary to public belief, this change of scene can actually improve retention because the knowledge becomes associated with multiple environments rather than tied to just one. Any room is fair game, as long as there's a suitable surface. Consider the living room, dining room, kitchen, bedroom, office, porch, or even a picnic table.

When in the workspace, the student should keep her backpack, schoolbooks, and assignment notebook or datebook nearby. Try to keep anything related to school centralized so that everything is in a school locker (if the student has one), in her backpack, or on one or two particular surfaces at home. Students should not have to search all over the house to find papers or run the risk of forgetting them under the day's newspaper.

TUTOR TOOLBOX

If your child does schoolwork while sitting on her bed, consider
providing a lap desk. It's not that convenient for tutoring sessions
but useful for individual work.

THE IMPORTANCE OF A
TUTOR SUPPLY KIT

Let's say it's your turn to make a salad for dinner. That should be easy
enough, no more than a ten-minute process. But there's a problem—
you can't find a cutting board, vegetable peeler, knife, or the veggies!

After much searching, each turns up in a different place: The cutting board in a hamper. The peeler in the hall closet. The carrots under
a bathroom sink, and the tomatoes in the tub. You never find the knife,
which means you end up with fork-cut tomatoes and too-large, hand-
broken carrot pieces.

Two hours later, you have a mediocre meal and a resolution never
to enter the kitchen again. Because of your disorganization, your "easy"
salad prep has been fraught with stress and only yielded a so-so product.

Now imagine that you end up in this situation, and it's your first
time *ever* making a salad. How much longer would the whole process
take? How much more frustrated would you feel? How would you end
up thinking about the process of making salad?

Your child is that novice salad maker. But instead of needing recipe
ingredients, he needs school supplies. How much time and energy does
your child waste looking for clean paper and sharpened pencils or using
subpar substitutes?

You can avoid this source of frustration if you **keep supplies for
your child in one place**. Consider designating a drawer, desk, or shelf as
the place where everything stays put.

Certain supplies should be duplicated throughout the home. Keep
writing implements in every room so that a pen or pencil is never more
than a few steps away.

For the sake of simplicity, Janna Taylor of Mind Full Tutors suggests that families put academic supplies in a tutoring kit that parents and children can move from room to room.

Here are some of the benefits of a **portable tutor supply kit**:

1. Your child can work in any part of the house. Every surface doubles as an impromptu learning or tutoring space.

2. You can take tutoring to go. At a moment's notice, your child can bring the kit to the yard, to a friend's or grandparent's home, in the car, or on vacation.

3. The kit serves as a signal that it's tutoring or work time. When the supplies come out, your child knows it's time to be productive.

When I worked at Potomac Tutors, in Potomac, Maryland, tutoring supplies lived in mobile breadbaskets. When the containers were not in use, the lids curved shut, neatly concealing their contents. You can also store goods in a colorful file box, Tupperware container, binder, or metal lunch box.

Stocking the Kit

The following are the should haves and could haves to keep in or near your mobile tutoring kit. Obviously, you can adapt these lists to suit your child's needs.

SHOULD HAVES

❏ Colored markers, pencils, or crayons

❏ Dictionary

❏ Extra graphite for mechanical pencils

❏ Folder or three-ring binder to hold special papers that have been produced during tutoring sessions and would be helpful for future review (for example, a list of formulas or a guide to the parts of speech)

❏ Highlighters

- ❏ Paper clips/binder clips
- ❏ Paper: lined and unlined
- ❏ Pencil sharpener
- ❏ Pencils
- ❏ Pens: black, blue, and red

COULD HAVES

- ❏ Book holder or any stand to vertically support a textbook or papers
- ❏ Extra folders
- ❏ Foreign language dictionary
- ❏ Glue stick
- ❏ Graph paper
- ❏ Hole puncher
- ❏ Hole reinforcements
- ❏ Index cards
- ❏ Manipulatives*
- ❏ Math tools: Might include a (graphing) calculator, compass, or protractor. Consider math fact charts (twelve by twelve

---

* As its name implies, a *manipulative* is something that your child can manipulate (besides you). These may include colored chips, flat movable shapes, tangrams, or stackable cubes. Besides being useful as creative playthings, they also help build basic math skills, including the ability to recognize patterns and understand the relationship between complex shapes. Raina Fishbane, the math resource teacher at Sidwell Friends School's Lower School, strongly recommends manipulatives as an alternative to "drill and kill" workbooks. Sidwell has students play with wooden blocks through third grade. Raina also recommends Cuisenaire Rods and base 10 blocks; the latter allow students to physically see numerical trades, such as by swapping ten "unit cubes" for a "ten rod" when practicing carrying in addition.

multiplication tables, for example). It's better for a child to refer to a chart than a calculator if need be, because the child will begin to see math patterns.

❑ Ruler

❑ Scissors

❑ Stapler

❑ Sticky notes for taking notes or little flags for marking notable points in readings

❑ Stopwatch, sand egg timer, or travel clock: For timed assignments or for use in creating deadlines as a motivational technique. The travel clock can be useful for when your child moves to a different workspace.

❑ Stress ball or beads

❑ Tape

❑ Tissues

❑ World and US maps: Even if there's a map or atlas nearby, stick a small folding world map and/or US map into your portable tutoring kit.

NEARBY

❑ Computer

❑ Printer

TUTOR TOOLBOX

For younger students, or anyone who enjoys using them, consider thicker writing implements and/or pencil grips.

REFERENCE MATERIALS YOU MAY WANT HANDY

❑ Almanac

❑ Atlas

❑ Globe

❑ Grammar handbook

❑ History textbooks

❑ One-volume encyclopedia

❑ Poetry anthologies

❑ Science reference books

You can find inexpensive textbooks on amazon.com, textbooks.com, half.com, and the independent bookstore finder indiebound.org.

Tutor Janna Taylor recommends setting aside a shelf for your child's school books. Make sure the shelf is in full view of the family, because this public placement of your child's "tools of the trade" validates his job, which is to be a student.

As I mentioned earlier, none of these supplies are universally required—and creative families on a budget can make do with alternatives. Again, Abraham Lincoln serves as an inspiring example. He could not afford paper or even a slate for mathematics, so he learned arithmetic by writing with charcoal on a shovel. He would scrape off his calculations with a jackknife between problems. Granted, your child

TUTOR TOOLBOX

Put colorful markers and highlighters in your tutor supply kit and use them when you map concepts or work through math problems. Brightness and variety can bring a subject to life. It can be particularly refreshing for older students, many of whom have spent years writing only in pen and pencil. Yellow highlighters do the best job of showing text. Other colors can be fun to use in different ways, such as to mark key passages with colored vertical lines in the margins.

may be at a disadvantage with a shovel and jackknife (unless she's in a fight with a kid who only has pen and paper), but she can still learn.

THE SIMPLE, SIX-STEP SESSION

So you've set up the workspace. It's uncluttered. You've got your portable tutoring toolkit fully stocked, with pencils sharpened. You even have your child present, so you are totally ready to tutor. What do you do?

Step 1. Signal Your Undivided Attention

Turn off your cell phone. If you're near a computer, close your e-mail, darken the monitor, and/or close the laptop. By cutting off outside communication, you are showing your child respect and modeling the behavior you want your own child to display when around teachers. Your child will see that there is a time when he is your absolute top priority—namely, when it's time to learn.

- **But I'm expecting an important call!** If you're expecting an unavoidable, important call—say from another child or your doctor or whomever—then keep your cell phone on vibrate. When the call comes, excuse yourself from the session to take it and then stay away for the shortest time possible. If it's not crucial, don't pick up.

- **I'm not *expecting* an important call, but what if I'm getting one and just don't know it?** That's why Alexander Graham Bell invented the answering machine, caller ID, and voice mail. Wait to see who is calling and what he or she needs before you commit to a conversation. Again, if you must pick up, speak briefly and request that you call the person back if it's nonessential.

If you think it would be fun, you can let your child help you decide who's worthy of your attention. For example: Obviously you would want to pick up if it's a child star search agent or J. K. Rowling on the line.

Speaking of phones, if your child has a cell phone, make sure it's off while you're working together or while he is working. Ideally, phones should not be used or even nearby during homework time.

Step 2. Greet Your Student

No matter what your mood, transmit to your child at least briefly that you are looking forward to the tutoring session—that it is truly a pleasure to sit down with her today. Try to engage her in at least one positive, nonwork-related interaction while allowing her the time to sit down, set up her own notes, and feel comfortable.

"Are you actually suggesting that I smile and greet my own child like some sort of stewardess on a 1960s Pan Am flight?" Yes. It may seem a little weird at first, this idea of making an effort to be polite and pleasant to one's own child. But think about it—children learn by example, and this is the way you teach your child to be polite and pleasant to others. And, more germane to the subject at hand, a pleasant beginning to your tutoring session will make the whole experience go more smoothly.

TUTOR TOOLBOX

Use thesauri and synonym lists with care. They can lead to stilted word substitution if students are unfamiliar with the words they select.

As part of your greeting, you might consider letting your child know how long you're planning to work with her today. Many children—and adults too—like to know when they start how long they'll be doing what they're doing. It gives them a sense of control.

Step 3. What's New?

This is the first of three core questions—"What's new?" "What's now?" and "What's next?"—that should guide your tutoring sessions.

Sit next to your child or at a 90 degree angle (on the other side of a table corner) so you can look at each other. If you haven't done so already, ask what's new in his classes. Do not ask *if* anything is new. Ask *what* is new.

If your child elaborates, great; if not, ask more specific questions: "What's the latest in your math class?" "What are you studying in world history right now?" Even if it's not a subject that you and your child will look at together, still ask. From your child's answers, you will get a sense of his academic interests, give your child the chance to reconsider the day's work, and give yourself the opportunity to drop any related references—"Oh, yes, I have a great-uncle from ancient Sumeria."

Find out: "What has happened since our last tutoring session?" "What have you learned?" "What have you added to your notes?" "What new questions do you have?"

For younger children, this is when they can show you the folder where they keep papers they're supposed to bring you. "Did you get any homework assignments back today?" Guide your child in filing these away now. For older students, make sure they've had time to put away the day's papers. You can also ask older students if they have gotten back assignments with comments from the teacher or any other academic news that they want to share.

Step 4. What's Now?

Of the three core questions, this one takes up the bulk of the session. You'll ask, "What do you want to accomplish today?" "What are your current assignments?" "Which of those would it be most helpful for us to review together?"

Toward the beginning of sessions, I often try to find out if there are any topics the student needs to know for her studies that are unclear. If there are, I encourage the student to talk through the topics to see if she can gain an understating on her own. Then (or sooner, depending on the case), I add my own explanation or find a resource that can clarify.

If the student has not found anything confusing, I go for a more open-ended approach. "Tell me what you know about [derivatives, the Vietnam War, the thermosphere] so far." This gives the student the chance to reflect on current material, to play teacher (thereby getting practice at communicating the information), and to discover new connections or questions. It also prompts a fuller conversation and often leads to additional research, a review of notes, and the ability for me (or you, as the tutor) to ask follow-up questions that will lead the student to develop a deeper understanding of the topic.

In general, I also like to find out what a child is reading in English class, what she thinks of the book or story at this point, and to whom she would or wouldn't recommend the reading (and why).

OPTIONAL PAUSE

You can pause your part in the tutoring session after step 4 to let your child complete homework assignments. Then you'd check in again for steps 5 and 6. Or you can carry on and finish all six steps, then leave your child to work independently, making yourself available if questions arise.

Step 5. What's Next?

If the three core tutoring session questions are Dickens's* three spirits, then this one represents the Ghost of Tutoring Sessions Future. At some point toward the end of your time sitting with your child, think

---

* Although "Dickens's" makes correct use of the apostrophe, tons of students (and some adults) get it wrong. A singular, possessive word that ends in "s" almost always gets an apostrophe and the letter "s" after it. If it looks funny to you, read *The Elements of Style* by Strunk and White and share what you learn with your child.

about how today's work leads to tomorrow's: "What are you working toward?" "What step logically follows this one?" "Once you understand this concept, what do you think the teacher will introduce next?"

If you haven't done so already, discuss the schedule for any long-term projects, review deadlines, check off completed homework assignments, and consider goals for the remainder of the day or weekend.

6. Quit While You're Ahead

As an elementary school student, I created a makeshift school in my room and, every now and then, managed to coax my preschool brother into attending. It was not a particularly fun school. Dan's one task was to complete math worksheets that I'd made for him. When he finished a sheet, I graded it, awarded him the appropriate color star sticker, and . . . gave him another worksheet. Instead of acknowledging when he'd reached his limit, I adopted the philosophy that four-year-olds just didn't know what was good for them and that he was lucky to have me for a teacher. Eventually, I came to realize that it's a bad sign for the future of a one-student schoolhouse when that one student has to flee, shrieking.

To avoid losing your student the way I lost mine, try to end the tutoring session on a high note. I think of this as quitting while you're ahead, which is what I should have done with my brother. Know your child's attention span and back off just *before* he fades. Deliberately leave your child to work independently after he's gotten a challenging problem right, not after he's bumbled through a problem and needs your help to figure out what he did wrong. If your session has been a struggle, see if you can finish by reviewing a slightly easier concept. You're not aiming to give your child a false sense of confidence—but you want him to think of your work together as a productive, positive time, one in which difficulties ultimately yield to progress. Give your child the feeling that when he works through assignments without you, he'll be able to push through and master them in the end.

Also, be sure to praise your child for his effort. In a way, it's the reverse-greet. Make it clear that you've enjoyed working with your child and that he should come to you or his teacher with any lingering or developing questions. Reference what you'll do next time—or, if you don't have a plan for next time, express your eagerness to sit down together for whatever you end up discussing.

TAKE BREAKS

Have you been sitting for more than fifteen minutes? If so, blood has pooled in your lower extremities. Lower levels of blood and oxygen are reaching your brain, and your working memory is suffering as a result. In short, your brain thinks it's time for bed.

TUTOR TOOLBOX

Sometimes your child will feel stressed or tired and want a break at a time when it's not convenient to take one (on a busy homework night or before a test). To be sure the brain is getting all the oxygen it needs to function optimally, students should pause briefly to take deep breaths and to drink water.

Some professional productivity coaches tell office workers to take breaks for ten minutes out of every hour. Your child should probably follow a similar schedule. In addition, it can be a good idea to take short breaks between taxing homework assignments so that the brain has time to process what has just been finished and prepare for a new subject.

Encourage your child to incorporate movement into his breaks. He should change his body's position, whether that means rolling around on the floor, running up the stairs, or simply stretching. Fatigued students might take a nap. Others might want to get a snack or beverage or to listen to invigorating music.

Along the same lines, make sure that your child has adequate transition time between school and afterschool homework or tutoring time. Of course, if he's motivated and ready to work when he gets home, that's fine as well. If students can walk home from school or play outside before homework time, that's a ready-made means of decompressing and of reinvigorating the mind.

TALKING TO YOUR CHILD

"How was school?" my mother used to ask my younger brother. He replied the same way each day: "School-like."

Your child's willingness to share information will vary based on his age, relationship with you, personality, and mood. Some students will be more likely to provide academic news than social news, and for others the opposite will be true.

Bland questions may produce lackluster results.

YOU: Was school good today?

YOUR CHILD: Yup.

YOU: Did you get a lot of homework?

YOUR CHILD: Nope.

YOU: Anything else going on?

YOUR CHILD: Nope.

YOU: Um. Okay. So, guess I'll see you later, when I'll ask you another set of unimaginative yes-no questions?

YOUR CHILD: Yup.

Ask questions that stand some chance of having interesting answers . . .

YOU: What are you doing in gym class?

YOUR CHILD: (*being annoyingly slow*): Ummm.

YOU: Jumping jacks? Sally's mother said something about that.

YOUR CHILD: Yeah.

YOU: And she said there was running and jumping. Oh, and archery and golf. And step aerobics?

YOUR CHILD: Yeah.

YOU: Why does Sally tell her mother everything? You're so *secretive*.

. . . but then give your child the time and space to answer your questions.

YOU: What are you doing in gym class?

YOUR CHILD: (*again, being annoyingly slow*): Ummm. (*YOU are nonjudgmentally silent*.) What did you ask?

YOU: What are you doing in gym class?

YOUR CHILD: Stuff.

YOU: Go on.

YOUR CHILD: Ummm. (*YOU wait patiently and silently*.) Oh, step aerobics.

YOU: What do you think about step aerobics?

YOUR CHILD: It's the reason we pay such high property taxes.

TUTOR TOOLBOX

If you don't want a yes-or-no answer, don't ask a yes-or-no question.

Look at what your silence has bought you: cynical humor! This and all other forms of sharing are well worth the wait.

Here are some possible conversation starters. Adjust the wording of these questions as needed to maximize the chances that your child will respond:

- "What's the most useful fact you learned today?" (or "What's the least useful?" and then challenge your child to think of an obscure situation where it *could*, theoretically, come in handy)

- "What's the next big school event?" (for example, the next speaker, holiday event, dance, or homecoming)

- "What's the most/least popular club/activity at school?"

If your child doesn't want to talk about a particular subject, don't force it unless you think something's wrong. If you're a helicopter parent, turn down the whir of your blades right now. Allow your child the courtesy of privacy. It's nice if your child chooses to share, but, just as your personal life is your own business, students are under no obligation to provide the details of their school lives. Imagine the torture of being forced to repeat the details of every day at work and every social engagement—don't put your child in that position.

Remember, your home is not a barbeque. Ask; don't grill.

IF YOU DON'T KNOW

Do admit it. That shows you're honest and transmits the message that it's okay to admit when you don't know something.

But don't be apologetic. That displays weakness unnecessarily and will erode a student's confidence in you.

YOU: So what do you know about algebraic distribution?

CHILD: You have to multiply something by something, but I have no clue what.

APOLOGETIC PARENT-TUTOR: I'm really sorry, but I don't remember anything about distribution. I wouldn't know where to start either.

Instead, have a plan.

> YOU: So what do you know about algebraic distribution?

> CHILD: You have to multiply something by something, but I have no clue what.

> PRACTICAL PARENT-TUTOR: I need to refresh my memory. Can I take a look at your notes on this?

You can read the notes silently while your child completes another task. If needed and if time permits, you can even review overnight and return to the material the next day. Alternatively, you can talk yourself through the notes aloud as your child observes, which sometimes can be enough of a review for the student that he'll be leading you through the material with expertise by the time you grasp it.

If you have at least a passing knowledge of a subject, it's often just as effective to suggest that your child take the lead right away.

> YOU: So what do you know about distribution?

> CHILD: You have to multiply something by something, but I have no clue what.

> YOU: Do you have any notes on it?

> CHILD: Yeah.

> YOU: Let's take a look at them. Talk me through them.

Then your child takes ownership of the process by talking through the notes. You *do not* have to understand algebraic distribution to do this step in the tutoring process. In fact, in any given subject, you don't need to be years ahead of your student—just a few minutes ahead. If you can read notes faster than your child, you're already there.

TUTOR TOOLBOX

What are the odds? . . . Did you know that math textbooks often have answers to the odd-numbered problems in the back of the book?

All you have to do is recognize whether the notes are clear and prompt the student to explain them.

CHILD: You write down what you want to multiply.

YOU: Do you get that step?

CHILD: Yeah.

YOU: What do you multiply here?

CHILD: It's "x + 3" multiplied by "x − 3."

YOU: Okay. So what happens next?

CHILD: I don't know.

YOU: What did you write in your notes?

CHILD: "X two."

YOU: What does that mean?

CHILD: The x and x become x two?

Now, you might not remember what *algebraic distribution* means, but here's where you might realize that your child has forgotten about exponents.

YOU: X times x is x *squared*. Your notes show that to multiply those two quantities, you first need to multiply the x times the x. And you get x squared.

> (*As needed, pause here to make sure your child understands the difference between adding and multiplying variables. Or review the material yourself first, saving the discussion for later.*)

CHILD: Oh. Right.

YOU: So if the x has a three next to it . . . ?

CHILD: X cubed.

YOU: Exactly. Now back to the problem. What happens next?

CHILD: You multiply everything else?

YOU: Is that what you did in your notes? Talk me through them.

And so on.

There have been so many times when I've not remembered a concept but it has come back to me or I've learned it for the first time as a student has explained it to me. Sometimes, just the act of reviewing her notes—which students often overlook as a means of studying—will be enough to help the student understand a concept.

If the student's notes fail, try the textbook, which often has nicely laid-out examples. Go through step by step, asking your child if she grasps the steps as you go along. Your goal is to pinpoint the step where your child's comprehension fails. Then you work through it, consulting relevant resources along the way.

If you know your child's work is headed in a particularly tricky direction, you can read ahead in the textbook on your own (another reason to have an extra textbook at home).

DITCHING DISTRACTIONS

Read these blurbs about the habits of famous writers and see if you can figure out why they're all in this section:

- John Cheever wrote in the basement of his apartment building, in a storage room without windows.

- Wolfgang Amadeus Mozart composed overnight, in bed.

- Marcel Proust wrote *Remembrance of Things Past* from a bedroom he'd soundproofed by covering the walls and ceiling with sheets of cork.

- Before the Greek orator Demosthenes prepared a speech, he shaved half of his head so that he would be too ashamed to be seen in public when he should be writing.

- Victor Hugo wrote nude. Apparently he instructed his valet not to give back his clothes until he had finished writing. Oh, and he was on the roof . . . in a glass cage.

What does a nude, caged Victor Hugo have to do with your children? More than you'd think.

Hugo is your children, and you are the valet.

Each of these writers was doing what your children need to do: eliminating distractions. Mozart worked during a dark, silent time of day, when most people were asleep. Proust blocked auditory interruptions. Cheever isolated himself from sound, light, and other people. By shaving half his head, thereby forcing his own confinement, Demosthenes effectively removed the human distraction as well. Hugo—well, it appears Hugo had a more difficult time, so he created additional obstacles, those being the roof, glass cage, and nudity. Then he did what you should encourage your children to do—he asked for help.

Again, in the analogy, you are the valet. You must manage your children's distractions (though please let them keep their clothes, and go easy on the cages).

Where They Do Take It All Away

For parents wary of the idea of taking away distractions from their children, consider this: There is a culture in America in which it is acceptable to forcibly separate students from distractions. Every single school night, students in this community lose access to televisions, iPods, e-mail, IMs, cell phones, and computers. They can do nothing but schoolwork. For hours. Every night. Silently. If they refuse, they are punished—even expelled.

Are these troubled children? Low achievers in isolation? Detainees in juvee?

No, quite the opposite: These are the children of academic privilege. They are the students of America's top boarding schools—Phillips Exeter and Phillips Andover, Choate Rosemary Hall and Lawrenceville, Georgetown Prep and Groton.

Groton's promotional video shows eighth-grade students at their study hours, sitting silently at spartan wooden desks as they do schoolwork from 8 to 10 p.m. Georgetown Prep, which enforces study hours from 7:30 to 9:30 p.m., says, "Study Hall provides each student with the discipline necessary to succeed academically."[2]

Not just recommended. "Necessary." This is one of the top schools in the country—where students must demonstrate motivation and academic superiority in order to get in. Even so, the school argues it's imperative that students have their access to distractions restricted in order to build strong academic habits. Here, supervision and denial are not a punishment. They're a privilege.

Prep school parents pay upward of $40,000 per year for their children to be deprived of distractions. Guess what: You, too, can institute study hours in your own home—for free!

Eve of Distraction

Every child is different, as is every child's reaction to potential distractions. With your help, your child can learn to recognize and remove distractions from her work environment.

Look at the following groups of distractions and ask yourself these questions:

- Which of these factors exist in the environment where my child works?

- Which of these factors are definitely distractions for my child?

- Which of these factors *might* be distractions for my child?

- Can I find a way to help my child eliminate some of these distractions?

- If so, which ones can we reasonably remove and which are unavoidable?

TECHNOLOGICAL DISTRACTIONS

This type of distraction may be most likely to creep into your child's study time, but, thankfully, it can also be the easiest to remove:

- Cell phone calls

- Text messaging

- Television

- Radio

- Facebook, Twitter, or other social networking or instant messaging
- E-mail
- Internet access

ACADEMIC DISTRACTIONS

- Learning disability
- Not knowing what to do
- Inadequate notes
- Disorganization, including messy folders or backpack
- Cluttered or unclean workspace
- Not reading directions or not understanding directions
- Unpredictable at-home schedule
- Unknown start or end time for work

PHYSICAL WELL-BEING DISTRACTIONS

- Hunger
- Thirst

- Fatigue
- Discomfort
- Too much comfort! (Some students work better at a desk than on the couch or bed.)

AUDITORY DISTRACTIONS

- Street noise
- Nearby conversations
- Music
- Ringing phone

SOCIAL DISTRACTIONS

- Sibling
- Parent
- Friend
- Pet

EMOTIONAL DISTRACTIONS

- Rewards
- Punishments
- Judgment by parents
- Competition with sibling or classmates
- Fighting parents or otherwise unstable home life

TUTOR TOOLBOX

If the Internet is a distraction, consider instituting "Internet out-age" hours in your home. You can deliberately, temporarily disable the Internet on any given computer or in your entire home.

- Bullying or other abuse

- Anxiety or depression

Let's Focus on Focus

When your child's working independently, see if any of these tricks help him to focus. Note that these are just ideas—pick only those that sound helpful for your family:

- Push the workspace table against a blank, solid-colored wall.

- Try the human equivalent of horse blinders: the desk privacy shield, sometimes called a desk privacy screen. Basically, these are large, trifold pieces of cardboard that stand on a desk surface and create three miniwalls, replicating the experience of being in a library carrel. (A baseball cap can also help reduce your child's range of vision.)

- Extinguish ceiling lights, thereby dimming distractions, and rely solely on a desk lamp, which will provide a spotlight for your child's work.

- When your student is bothered by noise while studying alone, she might want to try wearing wear earplugs. *Note*: For safety reasons, this should only be done when there is someone else at home.

- For students who want to listen to music, try instrumental pieces. Play anything without lyrics (or with lyrics in a language the student does not understand). This makes it less likely that the music will compete with language-based assignments.

- If your child needs to use a computer but finds her personal computer (if she has one) too distracting, she should try working on a different computer. Sitting at a family computer or a parent's work computer can make students less likely to browse websites or waste time. You can even deactivate the Internet during homework time or have your child type her assignment on a computer that predates the Internet (if available).

- Build consistency into your routine, especially if your work—
  or traveling between houses, in the case of a divorce—causes
  an erratic schedule. Have your child work independently at a
  school library or public library at the same time each afternoon
  before going home or before school each day. These locations
  are also effective for students who find their homes altogether
  too distracting.

If you won't turn off the TV (or eliminate another avoidable distraction), don't chastise your child for being distracted by it. Television
is designed to distract, and humans instinctively (for their own protec-
tion) pay attention to new stimuli. Telling someone to tune out a loud
sibling is like telling Dorothy and her gang to "pay no attention to that
man behind the curtain!" When the man behind the curtain is moving around frenetically and yelling into a microphone, it's unrealistic to
expect someone to ignore him.

NO SNOOZE IS *NOT* GOOD SNOOZE

Yawning, head drooping, my high-school student nodded off. I stopped
explaining and waited. He jerked his eyes open, clearly unsure about
how long he'd fallen asleep, then moments later nodded off again.

Another day, one of my tenth-grade students told me that she had
gotten about six hours of sleep the night before. She declared, matter-
of-factly, that this was "not bad." Apparently she regularly got less sleep.

I remember my own high school experience, at busy times doing
work until I fell asleep. When I woke up in the middle of the night, I'd
start again, until it was too hard to stay up, at which point I'd finally
"officially" go to sleep.

At a tutoring company where I worked, students deemed too tired
to work effectively were sent home; sleep is that vital to learning. The
National Sleep Foundation and the American Academy of Pediatrics
have issued recommendations for how much sleep students should get
each day. [3] (Adults should get an average of eight hours of sleep).

Age (years)	Sleep Recommended (hours)	Recommended Bedtime
5	10–11	Between 7 and 8:30 p.m.
6–12	10–11	Between 7:30 and 9 p.m.
13–19	8.5–9.5	Between 9 and 10:30 p.m.

Bear in mind that this is the *recommended* amount. As with anything else, every child is different. If your child seems to need significantly more or less sleep than this, it's worth asking his pediatrician about it.

There is one problem with these data: Studies have also shown that, biologically, teenagers naturally fall asleep at 10 p.m. or later. Given the early start time of many high schools, this means teenagers are chronically sleep deprived, which can lead to moodiness, trouble retaining and processing information, and even obesity. According to *NurtureShock* by Po Bronson and Ashley Merryman, when schools move their start times later, it has been shown to cut down on student–driver traffic accidents, improve overall quality of life, and even increase SAT scores. In fact, according to Bronson and Merryman, school performance tends to drop by two full grade levels when a student is sleep deprived. They also cited a study in which every additional *fifteen minutes* of sleep in a teen's habitual sleep schedule was shown to correlate with an increase in his or her grade point average of *one full letter grade*—not a bad exchange rate.[4]

Your child's health and well-being come first. If he's falling asleep at the table, suggest a fifteen- to twenty-minute nap and an earlier bedtime. Also, be aware that studies have shown that late-night exposure to the light from computer screens (and certain e-readers) can affect the body's melatonin levels, disrupting the sleep cycle. So for students who *can't* fall asleep at bedtime or don't feel ready to rest even if they're sleep deprived, a good first step is to cut down on computer and electronics use before bedtime.

FOOD FOR THOUGHT

Feeding kids nutritious food helps them play well and stay well. It also helps them *think* well. If you're trying to improve your child's scholastic performance, don't overlook the role diet can play.

For some students, food is a distraction—a plaything. "I bunned it!" proclaimed one of my young students as he pulled a flattened hamburger bun from between his chair seat and his rear end.

In your own child's case, observe whether food helps or hurts. For some students, hunger can be a bigger distraction than food itself. At lunch time, I encourage my high school students to bring plates of food into my office. I'd recommend providing a healthy snack to a hungry child. Make a beverage and easy, mess-free foods (e.g., carrot sticks) available during her session or homework time. The "mess-free" part is important. I met with one high school student who would bring an after-school snack of a drippy, handheld wrap. It's hard to complete your algebra homework when you're leaking chicken juice.

For Longer-Lasting Energy

When students eat high-sugar or insubstantial meals, their energy levels can fluctuate, dropping as soon as an hour or two after breakfast or lunch. This can make for an irritable, hungry, distractible student. Try making some of the following food substitutions (as per your child's dietary needs, of course), and see if your child can feel the difference.

Meal	Try to Eliminate ...	Instead, Try ...
Breakfast	• Cereal with an ingredient list that prominently features sugar or corn syrup, including sugary granolas and "breakfast bars"	• Low-sugar fruits: blueberries, blackberries, raspberries • Oatmeal • Whole-grain cereal with fiber • Nuts • Yogurt with wheat germ • Eggs
Lunch	• White bread • Sugary peanut butter	• Natural nut butter and honey or real-fruit jam • Whole-wheat or sprouted wheat bread • Apples and almond butter • Carrot sticks and hummus
Snack	• Gummy fruit snacks • Chips • Cheese puffs • Ice cream	• Grapes, strawberries, melon, oranges, clementines • Whole wheat frozen waffles • Pretzels • Roasted potato or sweet potato • Dried fruit, nuts (GORP, or good old raisins and peanuts) • Popcorn • Fruit-juice popsicles • Cheese
Dinner	• Pizza • Hamburgers • Hot dogs • Boxed macaroni and cheese	• Salad • Fish • Whole wheat pasta • Chicken • Quinoa with cranberries and nuts • Dark green vegetables: kale, spinach
Beverages	• Soda • Iced tea • Other sugar-based drinks	• Milk or milk substitute • Juice • Water • Blended fruit and yogurt

WHAT ABOUT ONE-ON-TWO TUTORING?

If you have more than one child, it's generally preferable to devote separate, individual time to each. But if your children do their homework in the same place, there may be times when you'll want to sit down and help when they're both (or all) there.

On the plus side, it can be motivating for a student to see a sibling taking his work seriously and engaging with you to discuss it. You'll also have the benefit of one child overhearing (and seeing) the content of the other's lessons, which means he might absorb portions of it. For some students, working near each other can even create a healthy level of competition and inspire both to show their dedication to academics. Homeschooling families sometimes find that younger siblings like to keep up with the older ones, thereby learning material that other students might not learn until later.

But be sure that your children do not get too competitive with each other. I once tutored tenth-grade twins who raced to complete their honors Algebra 2 work. They zoomed through the problems while sniping back and forth about the correct answers. One girl bragged about how quickly she got the answers, which made the second girl more defensive about her own work and less likely to slow down and ask questions when she had them. I knew that if I were to keep tutoring these students, I would need to separate them or ask them to work silently.

If you are tutoring more than one child at once, devote extra attention to ensure that each child is learning independently. When questioning one child, for example, don't let another child blurt out the answers, unless that's part of the activity.

Don't compare students to each other with the aim of making one feel less worthy than another. If you say, "Look how thoroughly your brother checks his math problems," consider later balancing it with, "Isn't your sister being conscientious about annotating her history notes?" And make sure your interactions with one child aren't so distracting that they make it more difficult for your other child to work. If that's the case, see if you can create separate work spaces for each child—or, at the very least, bring one child to a different location when you're working aloud with him.

TUTOR TAKE-AWAY

- Create a clean, clear, uncluttered workspace where you and your child have equal access to the space.
- It's helpful to have a well-stocked, *portable* tutor toolkit.
- Begin your tutoring session by signaling your undivided attention to your child.
- Tutor with three questions in mind: What's new? What's now? What's next?
- If you don't know, say so.
- Sometimes good tutoring means putting someone in a room and taking everything else away. In other words, minimize distractions.
- It pays to take breaks.
- Help your child to eat smart—maximizing nutrition optimizes scholastic performance.

CHAPTER 3

Mindset over Matter: Thinking Like a Professional Tutor

So you've mastered the tutoring trifecta (new, now, next), have stocked your workspace with office supplies, and have grasped the basics of a traditional tutoring session. Now it's time to refine your mindset to replicate that of a professional tutor.

TUTOR TO-DOS

Adopt the following three big-picture principles and you'll go a long way toward providing your child with motivation, reassurance, and a sense of academic control.

Love Learning

If you get nothing else from this chapter—if you get nothing else from this entire book—at least follow this one rule: show your children that *you love learning*. (If you don't love learning, for the sake of your child, pretend you do.) The easiest way for your child to become an academic success and a curious, mentally alert person is for him to *want* to learn. You are your child's role model and his main window into the world of

TUTOR TOOLBOX

Make sure there's laughter—or at least smiles—every time you tutor!

grown-ups, so if you value learning, your child will see that trait as a natural part of adulthood.

How do you model the love of learning during a session? Easy—show excitement as you talk about your child's studies. Get engaged. Your comments and questions should reference actual academic content, and they should do so with enough detail to show that you truly care.

- **Photosynthesis:** "Oh, cool. This is how plants breathe!"

- *Great Expectations:* "Isn't Miss Havisham's house creepy?"

- **Chinese language:** "I'm amazed you remember the stroke order. Can you teach me how to write a character?"

If your child expresses dislike of a particular subject, you can show that you sympathize, but then put a positive spin on the material. It may be hard to do, but try to think of the most interesting connection that comes to mind about a particular subject, even if it's goofy.

STUDENT: I hate fractions.

BAD PARENT-TUTOR: Then just finish quickly.

GOOD PARENT-TUTOR: Fractions remind me of pie. Would you rather eat two-fourths or four-eighths of a coconut custard pie?

STUDENT: The fall of Rome is so boring.

BAD PARENT-TUTOR: I never liked it either.

GOOD PARENT-TUTOR: Oh, hey, did you know that some historians had this theory that the entire Roman civilization collapsed because people were poisoned by lead in the drinking-water pipes?

GOOD PARENT-TUTOR: (*with slightly less knowledge*): I wonder what caused the fall of Rome. What do you think?

STUDENT: Why do I have to study Portuguese? That's not fair.

BAD PARENT-TUTOR: Life's not fair.

GOOD PARENT-TUTOR: What if Brazil invades America? You'll be able to translate!

Here are other ways to show that you love learning:

- **Value learners.** Whether it means making positive comments about the "nerd" character in a television show or praising the efforts of a neighbor who has decided to study gardening, send your child the message that you admire people who make the choice to investigate and acquire knowledge.

- **Ask follow-up questions.** Let's say Uncle Frank visits and talks about his interest in phrenology. Don't just go "Uh huh." Find out what phrenology *is*, why he started studying it, and whether anyone still really thinks that you can measure architectural talent by skull shape.

Exude Calm

Have you ever seen a baby learning to walk? Just when she thinks she's got it, she teeters and topples. Diapered bottom hits floorboards, and a stunned silence follows as the baby decides whether to giggle or scream.

How does the baby decide which to do? Her gut response is not to close her eyes and consider the relative pros and cons of crying ver-

---

TUTOR TOOLBOX

Adopt the pace of Nature. Her secret is patience.

—Ralph Waldo Emerson, in his "Education" lecture

---

sus laughing. Rather, she watches Mommy and Daddy for a quick cue. Savvy parents know the trick: An alarmed response—an "Oh no!" or a gasp—will prompt tears. The smiley "You're okay!" leads the child to respond in kind, with good cheer.

By the time this baby becomes a student, her reactions may be more complicated than a simple laugh or cry. Perhaps she will show her happiness with a smile and her stress with a racing heart rate, chewed-down fingernails, or insomnia. We age; we change. But what will stay the same, to a large extent, is that she will still get her response cues from you. This gives parents a source of power they don't always consider. So the question is, what behaviors are you modeling?

Take a typical high-stress academic dilemma: Your child comes to you, confused and upset. She admits that she has put off completing a big assignment until the night before it's due. Do you:

(a) Panic? This may include some or all of the following: raised voice, exclamations of exasperation, and the hysterical declaration that your child has failed her family, the state, and, possibly, God.

(b) Anxiously discuss the problem? You're nervous, and it shows. You share your sentiments with your child.

(c) Exude calm? You rationally discuss the problem and encourage a grounded, controlled response.

Exuding calm can be the hardest path to follow. It's also the most valuable. It's an attitude that says: "I'm not judging you. I'm on your side. You've learned your lesson, or at least you're in the process of learning it. Let's figure out what to do now."

Imagine that the child who procrastinated in this example grows up to study medicine. As an intern, she is engaged in a stressful surgery. She's working against the ticking clock, with two minutes left to remove an organ. Overwhelmed by the pressure, she freezes. "I don't know what to do!" she says, throwing up her bloodied hands.

The supervising doctor (her tutor) has a couple of options. He could panic and berate her: "I can't believe you got yourself into this mess . . . again! Now it's too late—there's nothing to be done! The patient will die! And you'll have to work at McDonald's for the rest of your life!"

He could anxiously attempt discussing it: "Eek. This is a really bad. Are you okay? I hope we can figure this out. I hope you don't mess up your career or the patient's health. Maybe you should try that maneuver again?"

Or he could choose to exude calm: "Put down your arms. Take a deep breath. What are you supposed to do next? Exactly—reach into the body cavity. That's excellent; now think about your next step. There you go."

Don't worry that responding calmly will transmit the wrong lesson. It won't. Just as the baby learned it hurt to hit the floor, the intern will know she's made a potentially dangerous error. She won't think "Excellent" means "I hope you freak out during our next appendectomy, too," just as your child completing a late assignment won't think, "Wow— Mom was supportive—I should always hand in homework late!" Guilt, a low grade, and the knowledge that you disapprove will take care of the lesson for you. The key is to show the student what she should do now that she's in this mess.

Tutoring is about considering *future* success as much as immediate success. Every assignment is an opportunity for learning about learning: Did I leave myself enough time for this assignment? Did I do enough research for this paper? As a result of my choices, was this assignment easy or hard? So many parents tolerate incorrect answers on an assignment ("Good try!"), yet throw hissy fits about the organizational and time management components, which can be just as challenging. Remember, in the same way that mistakes on math homework are okay because students learn by trial and error, mistakes in the approach— procrastination, poor time management—teach key life lessons and have their own learning curve.

Don't sabotage your child by teaching her to become paralyzed under stress. Keep in mind that, one day, your child may be in a situation with more serious consequences than a D on an overdue paper. If you panic at these little things, how will she react when big things go wrong? The key is to make sure that she knows how to get out of a mess without having a nervous breakdown—and how to avoid the mess next time around.

You can still be passionate and enthusiastic. You can even have a slight sense of urgency, though if you feel underlying anxiety and show it, your child will, too. But by exuding calm and talking through a crisis, you signal that even seemingly impossible tasks are manageable.

Break It Down

Which of these tasks sounds more manageable to you?

(a) Write a fifteen-page paper on Britain's Industrial Revolution.

(b) Walk to the library.

How about these?

(a) Win a spaghetti-bridge-building contest.

(b) Try to snap three different brands of uncooked spaghetti.

Or these?

(a) Construct a space ship and then fly it to the moon.

(b) Obtain a wrench and bolts.

In each case, (b) is one of the first steps needed to achieve (a). What's the point of these examples? When a task feels daunting, attack it by breaking it down into smaller, more manageable pieces.

Enough "breaking it down" and your child will start to independently "build it back up." Much of what your child now finds easy probably used to need deconstruction. Most likely, your twelfth-grader can solve arithmetic problems and write sentences without breaking these tasks down into steps. This was not always the case. For him (and for everyone else), writing a sentence as a young child probably meant struggling through a series of individual words. Writing each word was a conscious, letter-by-letter act, with each letter a stroke-by-stroke process. Gradually, your child built from letters to words and from words to sentences. Sentences may now be a cinch, but to complete larger projects, which might be intuitive for an adult, your child may require this same kind of breakdown.

For any large project, *de*construction is the key to construction. Breaking daunting, vague projects into steps makes the end goal easier to accomplish, meaning that students are less likely to get overwhelmed or procrastinate.

Let's say you have this big task: study for the final history exam. That's large and daunting. But if you turn it into a series of smaller steps, it starts to look more reasonable:

1. Find your history textbook and other readings. Find your notes from the year. Put them all on the table.

2. Get a yellow highlighter from your tutoring supply kit.

3. Sort your notes into three piles: (a) not needed for the exam, (b) might be needed for the exam, and (c) needed for the exam.

4. File (a) back in the binder.

5. Put (b) in a folder in your backpack. Tomorrow, ask your teacher about the (b) material's relevance to the exam.

6. Spend thirty minutes reviewing the oldest notes from (c) and highlighting key points.

Continue in this way to break down tasks. If the student writes out tasks in advance, he will also get the sense of accomplishment that comes from frequently checking off accomplishments. For children who get frustrated or lose focus easily, make the achievable tasks more frequent—perhaps he should be able to check off a completed task every fifteen minutes instead of every half-hour.

An episode of one of my favorite sitcoms, *The Office*, shows how helpful the step-creating process can be. When protagonist Michael Scott quits his job at Dunder-Mifflin Paper Company, he forms his own small business, the Michael Scott Paper Company. Pam, Michael's loyal receptionist, quits with him. On his first day of self-employment, Michael feels overwhelmed. Paralyzed by the vast, overarching task of creating a successful company, he instead cooks a tower of French toast.

Pam responds by making Michael a list of tasks, the first of which is to cook a giant breakfast. Lo and behold, task one has been accomplished! Michael has already achieved something on his list, and he begins to feel encouraged about the possibility of actually succeeding in his mission. It may sound absurd, but this approach works for people in the real world as well as on TV. There's no harm in creating steps that build in a sense of achievement for small or even *already completed* tasks.

If breaking assignments into steps is a new idea for your child, act as a guide. At some point, though, this approach should become second nature. If the method works for your child, you should eventually be able to say, "Have you broken it into steps?" and your child should independently be able to chop research papers, science projects, and even the college or job application process into bite-sized pieces.

Again, the goal is to break the big project into goals so small you can't help but achieve them. Or, said differently, break it down until it reaches a level the student can handle, and then stop. There's no point in thinking of each paper as a series of pen strokes if you already know how to write. If you break it down into tasks that are too small for the student, the project becomes cumbersome in a new way!

My graduate school advisor used to say that there's no such thing as writer's block—there's only not enough research. I think she's absolutely right, though I'd add to that. Sometimes writer's block (or homework block) comes from not understanding how to break a paper into paragraphs (or a project into steps).

In *Bird by Bird*, Anne Lamott's inspiring book about the writing life, she tells the story that led to her book's title. Lamott's ten-year-old brother had three months to write a big essay on birds. He procrastinated until the night before it was due, then froze under the enormity of the incomplete task. Lamott describes the reaction of her father. Instead of yelling, berating, or walking away to let his son wallow in a misery of his own making, Lamott's father "sat down beside him, put his arm around [her] brother's shoulder, and said, 'Bird by bird, buddy. Just take it bird by bird.'"[1]

This struck me for several reasons. First, the anecdote was an example of Lamott's father breaking a daunting assignment into a simple, easily understandable unit: the single bird. Second, the story implied that Lamott's father had not spent the previous three months hovering over his son's progress like a modern-day helicopter parent. While he may have offered assistance to his son throughout, he had given him the opportunity to handle the project on his own and, ultimately, to learn from his progress, or lack thereof. Finally, now that the ten-year-old had seen the consequences of not pacing himself, his father did not yell, panic, or lose control in any other unproductive manner. Instead, he exuded calm and, politely, offered support.

Within a written assignment, remember that students are not just writing one big glob of text. They're writing a series of paragraphs with separate points. This tends to be easiest to remember in science classes, where lab reports allow students to break their writing into labeled segments with clear purposes: "Hypothesis," "Procedure," "Results and Data," and so on. In other classes, the task may be more challenging.

TEACH YOUR CHILD OUTLINING.

Breaking down papers using outlines is a process I find helpful. One of my older students had to write a fifteen-page research paper about the difficulty of planning and constructing the Erie Canal. He read and researched, but then he got stuck. After a lifetime of writing five-paragraph essays, he had no idea what to do.

As the student and I discussed the problem, we came up with a possible plan that hinged on breaking up the big paper into smaller pieces. He could think of the fifteen-page paper as five minipapers, each focusing on an aspect of the canal's challenging creation: the political struggles during the approval process, the difficulties related to the nascent engineering industry, and three others. For each minipaper, the student would write a short outline. Then he would determine a logical order for the five outlines, after which he would come up with graceful transitions to flow from one theme to the next. Finally, he would reread the five outlines and related transition ideas in order, thinking about the subject as a whole, with an eye toward creating two additional segments—an outline for an introduction to the paper and a conclusion.

These steps would take some time. In fact, my student might spend a couple of hours planning before he would write a single sentence of his paper. But he would now have a complete guideline for writing the paper, which meant he could practically breeze through the writing itself. Perhaps he would even enjoy the writing process and, ideally, develop a sense of mastery over it. He would certainly be less stressed than if he had sat down in front of a blank computer screen and tried to craft a fifteen-page paper from scratch. What's more, by using this deconstruction and outlining process, he would be able to unjumble his ideas, to start to create something well-written, cogent, and thoughtful. And the ability to do that is one of education's most important goals.

NEW-TUTOR TRAPS

Yes, it's important to show you love learning, to stay calm, and to model ways to break down large tasks into little steps. But just as important as the tutor to-dos are the tutor to-*don'ts*. Read on to learn a few simple

---

TUTOR TOOLBOX

Whenever you feel like criticizing any one . . . just remember that all the people in this world haven't had the advantages that you've had.

—Advice from Nick Carraway's father, *The Great Gatsby,*
by F. Scott Fitzgerald

---

tutoring precepts that will help to keep your tutor–tutee interactions running smoothly.

Don't Assume

As a passenger in our family's Volvo, my younger brother, Dan, used to criticize sluggish drivers in front of us. "What's the matter with him?" he would ask, annoyed. My mother, herself an overcautious driver, usually defended the other driver. "You don't know," she would say. "What if he's slow because he's having a sneezing fit?"

Dan and I laughed at the idea that our station wagon was preceded by such a consistent cloud of allergens. It seemed as unlikely as my mother's other hypothetical musings: We had a cat who wouldn't stop meowing. We assumed he was pesky; my mother suggested he might be lonely. One of my classmates liked those button candies that came on long, white sheets of paper, but she also ate the paper with the candies. I thought she was hungry for attention—my mother suggested she might just be hungry. And I could not stand it when self-absorbed shoppers blocked the grocery store aisles with their carts, as if the whole world should wait for them. My mother, always sympathetic, suggested that some of these aisle-hoggers might not see us because of subpar peripheral vision.

At the time, my mother's theories sounded silly to me. But while I snickered at her then, I think like her now. Moreover, I find her mentality invaluable as I tutor. When you stop assuming and start considering the *why* behind the *what,* you can get a fresh perspective on another person's decisions. You become less judgmental and more tolerant, more able to empathize.

When I tutor, here's what I don't assume.

I don't assume that a child knows the basics. I found that high school students who studied the Berlin Airlift couldn't necessarily place the city in Germany. One of my students finished reading Chinua Achebe's *Things Fall Apart,* in which missionaries affect life in a traditional Nigerian village. On a hunch, I asked her if she knew what it meant to be a missionary. It turned out that she thought missionaries were mercenaries, or soldiers. I had a tenth-grade student who had noticed some days seemed to have more sun than others, but she hadn't realized that sunrises and sunsets were "scheduled" and that December's sunsets always came earlier than June's (in the Northern Hemisphere, at least).

My students' confusion reminded me of how easy it is for parents and tutors to make assumptions about what students already know. Now, if we're discussing a state, I ask students where it is in the country. If we're discussing a particular bill, I ask students to describe the two houses of Congress. Backing up to examine the bigger picture can be worth the time.

Katie McLane, the owner of Potomac Tutors, recalls her own learning process as she realized it was important to hide her surprise when students were lacking in material she considered basic. She remembers being shocked when students didn't know the rings in a tree stump showed the age of a tree. Another time, she was astounded when an eighth-grade student was adamant that California was on the East Coast. "You're going to appear really, really dumb if you don't know this," Katie said in response, stunned, then realized her statement sent exactly the wrong message. She had been trying to emphasize the importance of geography (a good message), but realized that her word choice and tone could have made this student insecure and unwilling to answer questions in the future. Now, years later, she's careful not to talk down to students who express misinformation.[2]

Not assuming is also valuable as a writing technique. In other words, you should teach your child that, when she is writing reports or papers, she should not assume that her readers know much about her topic. Remind your child to provide context for the reader, rather than assuming that a reader knows who wrote a book, where the story takes place, or what the characters do.

I don't assume that a child has necessarily heard everything that was said in class or seen everything that was written on the board. The reason I don't assume those things is simple: I think back to all the distractions I faced in school, even as a very focused student. Fire drills.

Hallway noise. Overcrowded classrooms. In high school physics class, I had to ignore the boy next to me, who regularly muttered factoids about assassins. Reviewing material after class often showed how much information I'd missed, which is exactly why a thorough study session can be so helpful.

I don't assume that any subject is too complex for me to review with a student. So often, tutoring means helping students follow steps so they can empower *themselves* to understand material. Even if your child's calculus class stumps you, the key to his comprehension may be tied to reading the section, looking through sample problems systematically, or talking through class notes.

Remember, you have an advantage: your child has grown up with *you*, not his teacher. Besides your child, you're the world's foremost expert on the words your child knows and the comparisons he will appreciate. A history teacher may be able to explain the intricacies of the Constitution with ease. But you're the one who knows that Great-Great-Aunt Sally was born in 1920, the year women got the right to vote.

I don't assume that tangents are irrelevant. Musings on other subjects can make your child's work relevant to real life. If you're clever, you can even take topics that seem hopelessly unrelated to your child's work and use them to your advantage:

YOU: Can you imagine what it was like to leave your house in Iraq during the US invasion?

YOUR TEN-YEAR-OLD CHILD: Can we go to the zoo?

YOU: *We* can, but think about Iraq. Bombs fall on a zoo. What happens?

YOUR CHILD: The animals die?

YOU: Maybe. What if the bombs hit the cages and the gates, but not the animals?

YOUR CHILD: The animals escape!

YOU: So, what do you think it would be like to leave your house?

YOUR CHILD: You'd have to stay away from lions—and bombs. It'd be scary.*

YOU: Exactly. Now, let's talk about . . .

An important point to remember is that your child hasn't absorbed all of your knowledge by osmosis. You and your child grew up exposed to different eras, teachers, and environments. As a result, your social and cultural references probably differ as well. When I got to college and tried out for the debate team, I had to make an impromptu argument about Reagan's 1983 "Star Wars" program (the Strategic Defense Initiative); I had no idea what it was. When the movie *MILK* came out, I was surprised to realize that I'd never heard of Harvey Milk before; he'd been assassinated in 1978. There's often a gap of ten to twenty years right before and after you were born that you don't know anything about—anyone who lived then takes knowledge of the period for granted, but the era is not yet removed enough to be in the history books. It's a historical blind spot.

No question is stupid. No matter how ridiculous a question may sound—or how obvious the answer may seem—if a student is asking you in earnest, you should not chastise, judge, or mock in response. Take any request for information seriously.

You never know what someone will not know; at times, the trouble may come from a simple misunderstanding. My husband still talks about the time his second-grade teacher gave the class a worksheet with a series of questions about wasps. Adam had never studied wasps and didn't know the answers, so he guessed his way through the paper and ended up with a low grade. Much later, he realized that he should have read the paragraph at the top of the paper—a paragraph full of information about wasps. Because his teacher had not mentioned the paragraph, Adam had assumed it was unrelated to his task; his teacher, on the other hand, had assumed everyone would intuit the connection.

---

* Incidentally, four lions really did escape from the Baghdad Zoo in 2003. Brian K. Vaughan and Niko Henrichon have written *Pride of Baghdad* (Vertigo, 2008), a graphic novel based on the story. It's most appropriate for high school students.

Sometimes you can spend years overlooking something that an outsider, or even another person in your position, would find instantly obvious. My mother didn't know that her father had a Polish accent until she was in her twenties and someone mentioned it to her. Plenty of New Yorkers never consider visiting the Statue of Liberty, though they may see it daily. I taught tenth graders at an Orthodox Jewish high school and found that some of them couldn't point to Israel on a world map. Embarrassing? Yes. Ironic? Yes. But so be it. We all have something that has never occurred to us before, perhaps because we have never asked about it or no one has ever asked us about it. If someone reacts to our ignorance with scorn or horror, we will be less likely to reveal or admit to areas of need in the future. Students who are judged by peers or parents may be less likely to ask and answer questions. So don't assume, and be willing to share information without scorn.

Remember that not making assumptions goes hand in hand with building patience. When you sit calmly behind a slow driver instead of honking or cutting him off, you telegraph that patience to your child. "So what?" you're saying. "There are more important things in life than getting there first. Maybe he's trying to figure out where to go. Maybe his toddler is having a tantrum in the backseat. Maybe he's just enjoying the day. So what? That's okay with me."

When you don't assume, you open your mind to creative rationales for frustrating situations. This translates into increased ability to see subtleties, interpret and analyze characters in texts, empathize, sympathize, and exhibit patience.

If you stop assuming, you can find out what your children truly don't know. Then you have your reward: you can help them learn so that the next time someone asks, they *will* know.

Don't Take It Personally

CHILD: I got an F on the chem quiz.

PARENT: Are you kidding me? An F?

CHILD: Sorry.

PARENT: I am very disappointed in you.

CHILD: O*kay.* I get it.

PARENT: And you'd better show some improvement in that attitude if you expect to me to keep paying for accordion lessons for you.

A good parent-tutor does not act dismayed or personally disappointed when his or her child receives a "bad" grade. Even if your child seems discouraged, it is not a green light to take a negative attitude. Believe me—every child in America knows which grades are most desirable, so there's rarely a need to point it out again. Instead, try expressing sympathy and encouragement.

CHILD: I got an F on the chem quiz.

PARENT: You did?

CHILD: I studied but all the wrong stuff!

PARENT: That must be really frustrating. What happened?

CHILD: I didn't know any of the noble gases. I mean, I thought I knew them, but then I forgot them *all.*

PARENT: Do you know what next week's quiz will be on?

CHILD: The alkali metals.

PARENT: How about if we come up with a way to help you remember those? And if it works, we can go back to the noble gases so you'll be sure to know them for the final.

It is rare for a student to get a low grade to spite his parents, so it should be rare for a parent to respond to a low grade with anger. Instead, adopt an attitude of understanding and a genuine interest in gauging your child's own reaction and helping accordingly.

When I managed a tutoring company, I often fielded calls from parents who were turning their children over to an outside tutor out of pure annoyance. They felt personally slighted by errors, foibles, and forgetfulness. My favorite comment came from the mother who said her son, an elementary school student, was more than she could bear: "I asked him to underline the subject, and he underlined the predicate just to annoy me."

Granted, it's possible this student was truly trying to bother his mother. But often, parents can overreact to legitimate mistakes. "Didn't we *just* go over this?" parents ask students who have not retained a concept. "Were you even *listening*?"

Here's the thing: Not every child learns every concept the first time around. Retention of information is so much more complicated than that. Some students don't absorb concepts immediately. They may be busy processing other information. Or they may need more of a foundation in a particular area before new facts can be built on top. Perhaps a student thought she understood a concept but was wrong. Consider how frustrating it can be for a student who struggles with memory. And sometimes, of course, students just aren't paying attention. Successful professional tutors do not express annoyance at these students; instead, they help students figure out why they struggled with concepts—and what can be done to understand and retain them going forward. As a parent-tutor, you will have a much better working relationship with your child if you adopt the same mentality.

In *The Hobart Shakespeareans*, a documentary about famed teacher Rafe Esquith's incredible fifth-grade Shakespeare troupe, one boy tells how a fourth-grade teacher labeled him a troublemaker, assuming his endless questions indicated that he wasn't listening. Esquith, on the other hand, would repeat explanations "even if it takes a thousand times," the boy says. Now, the fifth-grader was flourishing, even playing the lead in the year's play, *Hamlet*.

Don't Talk Down to Your Child

Why not talk to your child like he's an adult? "Uh, because he's *not* one?" you say. Yes, but if you speak to him as if he is, won't he then be more likely to learn to speak, write, and think like one? And aren't those some of the ultimate goals of his education?

I believe in talking to children as adults—to the extent that it's appropriate, of course; I'm not going to try to engage a five-year-old in a discussion about the Federal Reserve. But I *would* say to a five-year-old, "I'm contemplating stopping at the bank today, before we go to the park," without caring that he doesn't know what "contemplating" means. My using the word will help him figure it out and eventually be able to use the word himself. Besides, my addressing him in an adult tone conveys my respect for him, which yields good results.

MOTIVATIONAL TRICKS OF THE TUTORING TRADE

All of the above advice is well and good, you may be thinking, *if* your child is cooperating. But what about when she's resistant, moody, or simply unmotivated? Here are some tips and tricks that professional tutors use to motivate children.

Win-Win

Give the resistant child two options. This gives her a sense of control. The catch: Have both options lead to results you endorse.

NO

YOUR CHILD: I don't wanna do the math homework.

YOU: You have to.

YOUR CHILD: No.

YOU: But you *have* to.

YES

YOUR CHILD: I don't wanna do the math homework.

YOU: No problem—take a break from it! Do you want to work on spelling or world history?

YOUR CHILD: Spelling!

This method works for some children. Others can see through it and require more advanced tactics.

YOU: No problem—take a break from it! Would you rather switch to spelling or world history?

YOUR CHILD: Neither!

YOU: Would you rather finish your homework early and come to the puppy carnival with me tonight or take a break now, finish your homework later, and go to bed when you're done?

Please note: This is not an example of using a reward, which I don't endorse. This example assumes that you personally would be going to the puppy carnival regardless of your child's academic progress.

Reverse Psychology

- You probably shouldn't read this section.

- If I were you, I'd stop after this sentence.

- I can't imagine you'd be interested in the next paragraph.

Still here? Reverse psychology is when you tell someone to do (or not do) the opposite of what you want.

I actually have mixed feelings (appropriately enough) about this method. Be careful it doesn't backfire. The danger of luring students into doing something by saying, "You probably won't like this anyway" or "I wonder if you can handle this problem" is that a child might (1) agree or (2) think you're doubting her competence.

When tutoring, I prefer to put a positive spin on this technique. When a student makes a negative statement that has the potential for a negative response, I like to respond with a nonchalant—even supportive—attitude, with the goal of getting the student to reverse his own psychology.

I worked with an intelligent eighth-grade girl. She was a good writer, but when I prompted her to make changes in a draft of an essay, she made a provocative statement: "I don't revise."

My instinct was to respond with horror. But when I saw that her statement was a challenge and perhaps an assertion of independence,

I realized that pushing the issue would be a big mistake. I changed tactics. "Okay," I said. "It's your paper." Looking a bit surprised, but satisfied, my student went to her computer to print the paper.

I casually picked up her draft and read the beginning. "This is well-phrased," I said.

She looked up from her computer. "Thanks," she said.

"And I like how you—oh, wait, did you mean to leave out a comma here?" I asked, almost as an aside. And then, musing to myself, "I think you probably meant to include one, since it's a series."

She skimmed the computer document to see what I meant. Soon enough, as I alternately complimented and critiqued her paper, she was making changes throughout. This initially resistant student ended up learning to edit.

The Lure of the Taboo, Controversial, or Icky

A variant on the reverse-psychology gambit is to tempt your child with taboo. Want your child to read a book? Try banning it first. Tales of oppressive authority figures motivate students like nothing else: "What do you mean, we're not *allowed* to read the original, unabridged version of *Les Misérables* in French II? I'll show them!"

When my ninth-grade health teacher told us that some schools thought students "shouldn't" learn about drugs, we gave her our full attention. If only algebra were forbidden, we'd have math whizzes everywhere. It's possible you could even motivate a reluctant female student by making her aware of countries where girls are forbidden to attend school.

When I tutored students from a public high school in Maryland, I worked with a ninth-grade girl who was reading *The Catcher in the Rye* and was terribly uninterested in the book. "Really?" I said and then, whispering, "Didn't your teacher tell you about Salinger?"

"What do you mean?" she said.

I hesitated, wondering aloud (deliberately) whether I should tell her the truth about *The Catcher in the Rye* and Salinger, given that her teacher was trying to shield her from the truth about the book.

"What is it?" she said. "Tell me."

Who wouldn't want to read *Catcher in the Rye* knowing it's a favorite of psychopaths and that J. D. Salinger lived as a recluse in New Hampshire, eating little more than raw nuts, frozen peas, and lamb burgers cooked at no more than 150 degrees?* It worked for this student, who returned to her book with true interest.

When revealing "secret" information, you can hesitate for effect.

YOU: I'm not sure if I should—

YOUR CHILD: What? What is it?

YOU: It's just that it's . . . I'm not sure if it's okay to tell you . . . .

YOUR CHILD: Tell me! Come on!

YOU: Kiwi fruit used to be called . . . (*whispering*) Chinese gooseberries.

(Try that example before your child's next big test on tropical fruit.)

You can also use gross or icky facts to increase a student's interest in a topic that otherwise does not appeal to him. Vertebrates: Some lizards can escape from predators by detaching their own tails; while the rest of the lizard escapes, its left-behind tail *keeps moving*. Bacteria: The human body is made up of one trillion cells. How many bacteria live inside it? *Twenty trillion*. The digestive system: If you dissect owl pellets, you can find mouse bones. (In fact, you can buy owl pellet dissection kits if you want to investigate this at home.)

Try spicing up history with *A History of Private Life*, a five-volume series published by Belknap Press that covers 850 years (from the Roman Empire through the twentieth century) of the private habits of average citizens. Throughout, you can find details of home life, wardrobe, and even bathroom habits.

These are just a few ideas, of course. What icky facts would captivate *your* child?

---

* Read *At Home in the World: A Memoir* (Picador, 1999) by Joyce Maynard, for a fascinating depiction of Salinger.

Harness the Power of Narrative

Remember when your child was tiny and "Tell me a story!" was the constant demand? For the older child—and even for adults—stories still have appeal, and as a tutor you can use that interest to your child's scholastic advantage.

Let's say your child is learning about diseases. He's trying to remember that diphtheria is an "acute contagious disease treated with antitoxin." But he's bored and disconnected from the material; as a result, he's not retaining anything. "This has nothing to do with real life," he moans. But it does, and you can tell a true story to prove it.

"Back in 1924, the year your great-grandmother was born," you might say, "way back when Alaska was still a territory, and not yet our forty-ninth state, there was a doctor who lived in Nome, which was a remote region that ships could reach only in summer. Residents of Nome sometimes got sick with diphtheria, a fatal disease, but the doctor could treat them with a special antitoxin—meaning a substance that worked against, *anti*, the disease's *toxin*. But in 1925, the doctor's antitoxin expired, and it turned out there wasn't enough time for a ship to bring more antitoxin before the port closed for the winter. That December, a two-year-old child died of what the doctor believed to be tonsillitis. Then another child died, and another. Soon, the doctor realized the children were getting diphtheria, not tonsillitis, and that the contagious disease was about to become an epidemic, spreading and killing throughout Nome. In January of 1925, that doctor sent a desperate telegram to Washington, DC. Do you want to know what it said?"

You read the telegram and then tell about the twenty mushers and 150 sled dogs, including the now-memorialized Balto, who relayed across Alaska with emergency antitoxin to save Nome. This leads to a discussion of the diphtheria vaccine, which made antitoxins unnecessary, and the modern-day DPT vaccine that your own child probably received.

TUTOR TOOLBOX

Staring at his map of dead Londoners—and knowing that he might be next—Dr. John Snow began to notice that all the deaths were centered around one spot: the neighborhood water pump. . . .

Try listening to just the first line or two of someone's story *without* hoping to hear what happens next. It's hard to do. Stories get people's attention. Your child may not think she cares about cholera research from 1854, but she's probably going to want to know what Dr. John Snow found so interesting about the water pump.

Use narrative strategically to get and hold your child's attention.

"But, wait," you might be saying, "I wouldn't know this story! I didn't even know there was a story behind diphtheria."

There's a story behind everything. And these days, there's an easy way to find these stories: Googling. A simple Google search of the term "diphtheria story" would have yielded this one.

Biographies, autobiographies, and historical novels, such as *Johnny Tremain* (about the American Revolution) and *All Quiet on the Western Front* (about World War I) are a more traditional way of accessing story power to learn about the past. *The History of US*, a series by Joy Hakim, and *The Story of the World*, a series by Susan Wise Bauer, also do a great job of teaching through narrative.

MEET YOUR CHILD WHERE HE OR SHE IS

When I worked for a private tutoring company, tutor applicants had to answer this question: "What does it mean to you to 'meet a student where he or she is'?" At first, it sounded like a question of location. "It means to go to the student's home for appointments," I imagined the applicants responding. But that wasn't it—especially not in this case, as all our tutoring appointments took place on-site. Rather, the phrase meant that a tutor should adjust his or her instruction and expectations to meet a child's needs.

I saw this concept illustrated recently on an episode of the drama *Parenthood*. Max, an eight-year-old with Asberger's syndrome, insisted on regularly wearing a pirate outfit, even to school. His father was adamant about addressing this, and he regularly put his effort toward trying to convince Max not to dress like a pirate, to no avail. Gradually, Max's father saw that, by not acknowledging his son's current inability to change, he was causing conflict and giving up the opportunity to mentor his son in other areas. And so, by the end of the episode, Max's father had decided to meet his son where he (Max) was comfortable, and when he joined Max in the backyard to play, he, too, was dressed for swashbuckling, wearing a bandanna and toting a tennis-racket sword.

Hook Your Child

The mother of one of my first-grade students let me know that animals were his "hook." I had struggled to get this student to sit and write, but once I told him we were going to write a story about an animal, his attention span quadrupled. Suddenly he was composing a story about the adventures of Sizzle the Snake.

Students learn to start papers with a hook to catch readers' attention. Likewise, I think every child—yours included—has at least one hook. Your task is to find facts and anecdotes that can both appeal to your child's interests and remain relevant to the academic topic at hand. As your child's range of knowledge broadens, he will be able to make these connections more easily, but, for now, your adult expertise will make the process easier.

Think about what interests your child and find ways to relate those interests to her current studies. It's okay if the hook-related information is only loosely tied to your child's work or if it's a little silly, as it encourages students to draw creative connections between fields. If baseball is the hook, talk batting averages before a review of mean, median, and mode. For a musical student, play the *Jekyll & Hyde* musical soundtrack before your child reads Robert Louis Stevenson's *The Strange Case of Dr. Jekyll and Mr. Hyde*. Heck, if your child adores grapefruit but hates US history, look up grapefruit-related dates; tell her about when the grapefruit first came to Florida (1823) as a lead-in to a reading about when Florida became a US territory (1822). When you personalize information like this, you're showing that a large area of knowledge has practical, smaller-scale applications, you're teaching your child to be creative in making connections between topics, you're modeling the kind of flexible thinking that innovators and world-changers employ when solving problems—and your child has more fun, too.

TUTOR TAKE-AWAY

- One of the best things you can do for your child is to model a love of learning.

- Cultivate calm.

- When confronted with complex assignments, it helps to break them down.

- Teach your child to outline.

- The best tutors keep assumptions to a minimum, and they don't judge.

- Don't take things personally.

- Don't talk down to your child.

- Create win-win options for your child.

- Try using reverse psychology.

- To spike your child's interest, consider the controversial.

- Tell stories.

- Where your child *is* is more important than where you'd like him to be.

CHAPTER 4

Feasts, Field Trips, and Froebel: The Creative Parent-Tutor

I had lost him. My very active first-grade student had just slithered off of his chair . . . again. He was supposed to be practicing writing letters, but nothing seemed to interest him less.

I had already tried every tactic I could think of to keep him engaged—even, as a last resort, offering that he could sit next to his homegrown tomato plant. But my attempts had failed, I concluded, given that he now lay collapsed under the dining table.

"I need you to come back up here on your seat so we can keep working," I said, peering under the table.

He gave me an incredulous look, as if I was inconveniencing him (which I suppose I was) and should have known better. "I'm cleaning the dirt from between my toes," he said.

"You're cleaning the dirt . . ." I echoed.

"It's on my list!" he said adamantly.

His list? "What a list that must be!" I thought. "'Poke frog. Pick at scab. Collect belly button lint.'"

"Well, you know what's on my list?" I said, rather uncreatively. "Getting you to sit in your chair!"

My student did sit and focus—eventually. He had practiced a few of his letters, and for that I was glad. But then I thought about how he had grimaced as he worked, checked the clock every few seconds, and fled from me at the end of our session. I wondered whether a tutoring session that inspired this level of reluctance could really be considered a success. But what else could I have done? After all, here I was trying in vain to get this kid to write, and he was cleaning the dirt from between his toes because it was on some imaginary list.

And then it hit me. His *imaginary list*, probably filled with satisfyingly gross kid activities. What if, instead of ordering him to return to his letter-writing drills, I had helped him compose his to-do list? I could have written my own ridiculous list ("Bake troublesome students into meat pies") and asked him to try to read the words—or letters, at least—aloud, and then we could have laughed at the silly tasks. My student had presented me with the perfect tutoring activity. And I had ignored it.

In yoga and other movement classes, instructors offer "modifications" based on students' individual bodies and level of expertise. This kind of variation allows students to meet their separate needs while working toward the same goal. Why should academic learning be any different? The same teaching style does not work for everyone, and why should it?

There are so many creative and dynamic ways for parents to fashion fun and for children to learn information that might be presented more rigidly at school. Young children can study the alphabet by spraying and tracing letters in shaving cream. Older students can recite multiplication tables with movement, taking one step up a staircase for each number in the series. The whole family can role-play scenes to bring novels or historical events to life. The goal of this chapter is to help you think outside the box—better yet, to *jump* outside the box with your children, and to encourage them to crayon skyscraper windows on the outside of it. (Could also be useful as a way of learning multiplication; e.g., fifty rows of four windows each, on the outside of a refrigerator box, equals two hundred windows.)

There's nothing wrong with inventing new approaches to foster the learning process. In fact, plenty of esteemed educators have gone outside the conventional wisdom to come up with creative new ways to teach children. Let's look at some of them.

WHAT WE CAN LEARN FROM . . .

Montessori

Italian educator Maria Montessori advocated having different ages mix in the classroom. The older ones could model skills for the younger ones and reinforce their own knowledge in the process.

Since you may have different ages mixing in your home, why not take advantage of this concept? Have your seven-year old teach his six-month-old sister subtraction. No, this is not a misprint. Dub your active first-grader "the math professor" and have him demonstrate subtraction to his infant sister using her donut-stacker toy. He'll be improving his arithmetic skills, and she'll probably be delighted.

Or have your teenager, faced with an A.P. history test, teach the seven-year-old about American history. Both will benefit academically.

The Froebel Kindergarten

In the late 1830s, the German educator Friedrich Froebel founded the first kindergarten. Froebel recognized the value of free, imaginative play. When the kindergarteners weren't busy singing or gardening, they were using Froebel's Play-Gifts, a series of six gifts (a number that has climbed posthumously) comprised of simple yarn balls and increasingly complex wooden blocks. Frank Lloyd Wright is among the architects said to have been inspired by these gifts. Kindergartens don't generally use Froebel's gifts at school nowadays, but you can find them for use at home.

By the way, *kindergarten* means *children's garden*, and the emphasis was on playing in one's garden, or play-space, not on filling in worksheets. Worksheets are fine for those children who love to fill them out, but they shouldn't be overused with those five-year-olds who'd rather find out about the world by building with blocks or digging in the dirt.

The Waldorf Method

Austrian philosopher Rudolf Steiner developed Waldorf Education, a system that came on the scholastic scene in 1919 with the opening of the first Waldorf school. Today, Waldorf schools support guided, movement-based, tactile, imaginative free play. Waldorf-endorsed and -inspired playthings put an emphasis on simplicity and allow children to exert creative control as they put their toys to use:

Waldorf dolls. For both girls and boys, these soft dolls have movable limbs and extremely simple facial features, allowing children to imagine freely.

Playstands. These boxy wooden frameworks provide the skeletons of play structures that can be easily transformed into castles, caves, markets, pet shops, or puppet theaters with the help of a canopy roof, couch cushion drawbridge, or basic props. You can also use a large cardboard box for a makeshift playstand.

Play clothes. Waldorf's dress-up capes, shawls, and veils are often made of flowing silks. While you can certainly buy these materials, you can also fashion costumes from old sheets or towels.

Figures. These small wooden figures are painted whimsically to suggest animals, people, and fantasy characters. Use these toys to engage young children in creative mental play, prepping their minds for the flexibility and imagination that higher-level thinking requires.

Homeschooling

Though John Holt has been described as the father of unschooling, he's actually the father of modern homeschooling as well. His efforts in the 1970s spawned a network of at-home education experts nationwide.

No matter where your children attend school, you can still use many of the techniques that homeschoolers have popularized:

Lapbooking. A lapbook is the academic equivalent of a scrapbook. The labbook of a student studying Hawaii might include anything from pressed lei blossoms and postcards of pigs on spits to a historical map of Hawaii, a pull-out timeline of Hawaii's pre-US history, and a taped-in envelope of homemade flip-me-over Hawaiian/English flash cards.

Students of any age can create these themed books. They can be used short term, in conjunction with a particular novel or unit, or—ideally—longer term, as a fun reference manual for math concepts, scientific phenomena, or historical eras.

Aficionados have created "minibook" templates for use within lapbooks. Popular templates include the layered book, accordian book, and flip-flap book. A related trend, "notebooking," relies more on three-ring binders but also makes use of minibooks.

The four-year cycle. As Susan Wise Bauer and Jessie Wise explain in their book *The Well-Trained Mind: A Guide to Classical Education at Home* (W.W. Norton, 2009), a four-year educational cycle allows students to gain familiarity with concepts three times throughout their K–12 educational careers. For example, Bauer and Wise's plan has students reading *Beowulf* in second, sixth, and tenth grades. A simple, accessible storybook version builds familiarity and is followed four years later by an age-appropriate adaptation and finally, for the oldest students, by the original version. This technique improves retention, and because the students have become comfortable with the tale when young, the proposition of reading the original text in high school becomes far less daunting.

Timelines. Walk into the basement of Sarah Arikian's New York home, and you can follow a strip of paper that stretches around all four walls of the room, overlapping itself at the end. It's a timeline of world history that her homeschooled children created, featuring events from the time of Tutankhamen through Europe's Dark Ages to the American Revolution. A second timeline nearby features pictures of all the American presidents.

While wall timelines are common practice among homeschooling families, any student can create an at-home timeline, either on a wall or in a binder, to serve as a visual reminder of in-school lessons and as a reference tool. The Arikians found the timeline system to be most effective when each child had the chance to create her own timeline. Families can design their own timeline images or purchase them from companies that make educational timeline materials. (Be forewarned that some religious companies produce timeline materials that date the creation of the world at 4004 BCE.)

Hands on. Jessica Hulcy, the author of the KONOS homeschooling curricula, points out that students remember 80 percent of what they do and 20 percent of what they read. Homeschoolers are known for taking advantage of hands-on activities; for this reason, one of KONOS's signature tasks is having children build a giant model of the human ear under their dining table. Apparently kids love it. "They keep playing in their ear all afternoon," Hulcy says, "and then Dad comes home, and he has to crawl through the ear. It makes learning fun."[1]

In India, the hands-on principle guided the Riverside School when its teachers wanted to help its fifth-graders understand the lives of child laborers. Students were assigned to spend eight hours rolling incense sticks, a task that gave them a tangible appreciation for the difficulty of the work that children throughout India perform daily.

Find ways that your child can do, feel, and experience the concepts that she otherwise might read and forget. Learning about the era when African-Americans were forced to sit in the back of the bus? Get on a crowded bus and have your child find an open seat—better yet, get on an empty bus and have your child move to the back anyway. Your child may find the process of *doing* allows her to absorb a concept in a permanent, meaningful way.

Homeschooling community. Homeschoolers share education ideas at conferences, in online forums, and through specialized magazines— but non-homeschooling parents can also find advice in these sources. Start by checking out *Home Education Magazine*, *The Old Schoolhouse Magazine*, and the *Well-Trained Mind* forums (welltrainedmind.com/ forums).

Unschooling

Unschoolers take homeschooling to a whole new level of laid-backness. They let their children's interests guide the educational process. It may sound unconventional (it is) or risky (isn't everything?), but unschooling can help children retain the passion for learning that is key in tutoring and education.

Field trips. Why learn from a textbook when you can educate yourself by seeing and doing? Visit historic homes, battlefields, museums, zoos, aquariums, farms, factories, and parks. Stay local or travel farther afield; catering trips to the preceding, current, or upcoming year's course of study. Learning about John Adams? Visit Peacefield in Quincy, Massachusetts. Geology buff? Set out for Zion National Park's pastel cliffs to see the results of sedimentation.

Let's play! As unschooler Jan Hunt said in *The Unschooling Unmanual*, her son "learned about money by playing Monopoly, about spelling by playing Scrabble, about strategies by playing chess, Clue, and video games, about our culture by watching classic and modern TV shows and films, about politics and government by watching, 'Yes, Minister,' about grammar by playing Mad Libs, about fractions by cooking, about words by playing Dictionary, and writing skills by reading P. G. Wodehouse. He learns about life through living it."[2] Unschooling parents are adept at finding innovative, nontraditional education materials to augment a child's natural focus.

TUTOR TOOLBOX

It is absurd and anti-life to be part of a system that compels you to sit in confinement with people of exactly the same age and social class.

—John Taylor Gatto, *Dumbing Us Down*

Traditional school systems may also advocate playing games. Math teacher Raina Fishbane laments the lack of understanding she has seen when questioning students who rely on learning through rigid drills. "Oh, we haven't gotten to the 8s yet," said a student who was learning multiplication by memorizing flashcards rather than internalizing concepts. Raina tells parents to supplement school math work by playing games such as Twenty-One (cards), Mancala, and Othello.

Adventure and Imagination playgrounds. As far as I know, these types of playgrounds are not the work of unschoolers, but I mention them here because they take advantage of the same spirit of open-ended creativity. At adventure playgrounds, of which there are two in the United States (both in California), "playworkers" fuse play and work by helping visitors craft raw materials into tree forts, river rafts, and whatever else they invent.

Imagination Playground also emphasizes "child-directed, unstructured free play."[3] At the Imagination Playground in New York's South Street Seaport, children use "loose parts" comprised of foam blocks, noodles, and balls; sand; and water to design their own playspaces.

Besides visiting these playgrounds or creating a similar environment in your own yard, you can collect "loose parts" for indoor projects. Think of yourself as your child's personal playworker, with your role being that of the facilitator who helps build the craft your child wants to steer.

A POTPOURRI OF THE PLAYFUL

Here are some more ideas to get your creative juices flowing. Of course, not every approach will work for every child. But if you find just one new technique effective, it may make a world of difference in how your student feels about schoolwork.

Don't Act Your Age!

Every once in a while, find an activity that seems not to be age-appropriate for your older kids or teenagers—for example, fingerpainting, coloring, or reading picture books—as a way of loosening up their learning experience.

Likewise, have little kids perform traditionally adult activities, like making business cards for their favorite animals or choosing supplies to carry in a briefcase.

Move It!

I once worked with a fidgety first grader who begged his mother to hold him upside down by his feet while I showed him flashcards. "Count them!" he proclaimed as his mother set him back on his feet. He was gleeful when he found out that he had read seventeen words, then fell into a living-room chair.

As a parent-tutor, you are trying to help your child find the learning style that works best for him. Incorporating movement provides the stimulation that many students need to keep their bodies and brains active, whether they are kinesthetic learners or just healthy, active kids.

So let your child pace. Jump around. Sit on an exercise ball while working. Read while sitting or lying in a hammock. Take a break to jump rope. At the beach, write in the sand.

TUTOR TOOLBOX

Try to incorporate movement into review. Try a Math March on the stairs for the multiplication tables. Tell your elementary-school child to climb a stair each time she counts up (7, 14, 21 . . .) and descend a stair each time she counts down (84, 77, 70 . . .). See how fast she can go—holding on to the banister, of course.

Walk in the shape of the trickiest spelling words. If your child keeps spelling a word with an "e" rather than a "u," have him walk in the shape of a "u" while repeating the word. (Be careful with the most circular letters if your child is prone to motion sickness. . . .)

Tired of graphing on paper? Use sidewalk chalk to draw an xy-axis on the sidewalk, using a board or the side of a garbage can as a ruler. See if your child can jump between coordinate points—from (4, 2) to (-2, -8), for example. Can your child roll a ball along the line $y = x$? What about pushing it along the graph of $y = x^2$? Ask your child to set up dominoes along the equations of several lines. Then allow him to topple the lines that are set up correctly.

The Peripatetic Parent: Take a Walk

When he lived in Newington Green in the early 1800s, John Stuart Mill took daily prebreakfast walks with his father during which they discussed the history lessons Mill had read the previous day. My mother, too, walked me with me, and it was a routine that provided us with a guaranteed time to talk. Try incorporating a walking routine into your and your child's lives. You might find that your child begins to share more or communicate in a different way when you engage him in regular strolls.

FOOD, GLORIOUS FOOD

Three meals a day. That's 1,095 meals a year. Assuming a thirty-minute meal (overestimating for breakfast but compensating for not including snack time), your child probably devotes five hundred hours a year to eating. Besides providing him with bodily nutrients, see if you can also use that time to nourish your child intellectually.

Feasts for the Mind

Studying ancient Egypt? Have your child research and prepare the foods the ancient Egyptians ate. Perhaps you'll decide to celebrate the Feast of Wagy, the January 17 "day of the dead" that honors the god Osiris. You'll eat fish- and egg-based dishes, turnips, grapes, figs, and nut-stuffed and coconut-coated dates. Your children may be inspired to create hieroglyphics-laced menus or eat dinner wearing linen clothes and sandals.

Your child can invite friends to help cook or eat the food. He might want to ask the classroom teacher whether the class would appreciate samples—themed food sometimes ends up being a good extra-credit project.

As another historical tie-in, serve a president's or other historical figure's favorite food. There's always cherry pie in honor of George Washington's supposed admission of chopping down the tree. You can also use *The President's Table* by Barry H. Landau to replicate menu items from inauguration meals and hunt online for foods served at other historical high points (or lows, as in the case of the meal before the sinking of the Titanic).

Ask your children to solve culinary mysteries. What was in the "three delicacies with egg-white" that President Nixon ate at a dinner he hosted in Beijing? What's the story behind the Titanic's "Waldorf pudding"?

Order freeze-dried space food and have an astronaut-style meal when NASA sends up its next mission. For dessert, have your child try chunks of chalky astronaut ice cream.

You can celebrate studying the geography, culture, language, or historical period of a particular country by going to a related restaurant. Discuss the Great Wall over Chinese dim sum, plan a trip to visit the cherry blossoms while maneuvering chopsticks over Japanese sushi, and mark Bastille Day at a creperie. For a (quasi-)eleventh-century experience, check out Medieval Times, where you can eat chicken legs with your hands while watching knights joust on horseback.

Teaching Kids to Play with Their Food

Playing with food is only a waste if you have to throw it away when you're done. As long as it all ends up in someone's stomach, you can safely think of play dough as your new Play-Doh.

Make a mushy model. Mashed potatoes, pudding, oatmeal, and other malleable meals are just asking for your child to mold them into the shape of your state, the Great Lakes, or the USA.

Bake educational shapes. You can make edible modeling dough. Better yet, make cookie dough and let children shape it into tasty creations. The smallest children can make animal heads and basic geometric shapes. Older children can craft rhombi and trapezoids, with the stipulation that they measure the area of cookies before eating them. For circular cookies (or pie), calculate circumference and area: $C = 2\pi r$ and $A = \pi r^2$ respectively.

Speaking of pie, it's also useful for learning to cut fractional pieces (as is any solid food, for that matter). Instead of saying, "I only want a tiny bit," ask for one sixteenth of the pie. (And don't forget to eat pie when you celebrate Pi Day on March 14, or 3.14.) Decorate cookies fractionally, with brown sprinkles on one third of a cookie and colored sprinkles on the remaining two thirds.

Use raisins, chocolate chips, and other decorating ingredients to mark the capitals on state-shaped cookies.

In "Cosmic Cuisine: An Edible Journey Through the Solar System" from a 2010 issue of *Home Education Magazine,* a mother describes the way her family used cookies to model the planets in our solar system, with Mercury needing the least baking time and Saturn the most. This allowed her children to see the relative size of planets. They used frosting and food dye to color the planets according to their surface type and bands. She suggested using licorice for the rings, M&Ms for moons (Jupiter needed sixty-three!), and Nerds candy for the asteroid belt between Mars and Jupiter. Then they measured how big a sun cookie would have to be—the size of their whole dining room!

AT-HOME IMMERSION: EDUCATIONAL THEMES

You may be familiar with language immersion, where a language learner is tossed into and surrounded by a foreign language for an extended period of time. The ringing of school bells hinders immersive academics and forces the end of a subject, regardless of how well the lesson was going. Even tutoring sessions with outside tutors are usually limited by time constraints. As a parent-tutor, you have the luxury of creating an at-home immersion experience in *any* subject, allowing a child to explore outside resources related to a concept of interest. You can be creative on a grander scale than a professional tutor. Immerse your child in a new concept or culture with a themed mini-lesson that spans a meal, evening, day, week, month, year, (birthday) party, sleepover, car trip, or vacation.

Let's say your young children express interest in bears. Read books from the Berenstain Bears, Paddington Bear, and Corduroy Bear series. Then find nonfiction books about polar bears and grizzly bears. Ask your children what would happen if polar and grizzly bears mated and then talk about the (real) "grolar" bear. Borrow documentaries about bears from the library. Go to the zoo and time your visit so that you can see bears being fed.

Exposure to a whole set of similar items allows students to start making associations and comparisons, and it teaches them critical thinking and comparative skills. You can prompt the development of these skills with questions: How do Stan and Jan Berenstain's bears look? How does this compare with Paddington and Corduroy and with the bears in the zoo? Are panda and koala bears "real" bears? What else looks like a bear? How do you escape from a bear?

For a high school student studying *Pride and Prejudice*, go beyond the book. Listen to the compositions of Ludwig von Beethoven and other musicians who would have been known to Jane Austen or her characters. Watch and contrast the BBC miniseries and other adaptations and spin-offs, such as the Bollywood-style *Bride and Prejudice* and *Lost in Austen*, in which a modern-day British woman switches places with Elizabeth Bennet, who soon cuts her hair short and favors a macrobiotic diet.

MY VERY EDUCATED MOTHER JUST SERVED US NAAN (AND OTHER PLUTO-FREE "MNEW"-AGE MNEMONICS)

A *mnemonic* (memory) *device* is any trick that helps you remember something. It might be a fact. A person's name. The walking route to get home from school. The thirteen colonies. You probably use dozens of mnemonic devices and don't even know it. See which of the following topics look familiar to you.

- **Acronyms.** Acronyms are so commonly learned that for many people they're what spring to mind at the words *mnemonic device*. You probably learned the "name" ROY G. BIV, each letter of which represents a color in the rainbow's visible light spectrum (red, orange, yellow, green, blue, indigo, violet).

    One of my ninth-grade students remembered ACTG (the nitrogenous bases in DNA) only because two of the letters are

---

TUTOR TOOLBOX

The following are some popular acronyms:

- **FACE:** The order of the treble clef spaces, low to high (F, A, C, E)
- **HOMES:** The Great Lakes (Huron, Ontario, Michigan, Erie, Superior)
- **SOH-CAH-TOA:** Trigonometric relationships (sine=opposite/hypotenuse; cosine=adjacent/hypotenuse; tangent=opposite/adjacent)
- **FANBOYS:** Coordinating conjunctions (for, and, nor, but, or, yet, so)
- **MAIN:** Causes of World War I (militarism, alliances, imperialism, nationalism)
- **BASMOQ:** Canadian provinces bordering the United States from west to east (British Columbia, Alberta, Saskatchewan, Manitoba, Ontario, Quebec)

CG—CosmoGirl. (Actually, those may be the only two bases she remembered.)

- **Acrostics.** In acrostics, the first letter of each word in a sentence or phrase represents the first letter of a series of words you want to remember. (See Tutor Toolbox, below, for examples.)

- **Alliteration.** My eleventh-grade English teacher used "long lines, quick quotes" to help us remember what types of titles to underline and which to put in quotation marks. "Long" or full-length works, such as books, magazines, plays, album titles, and TV series, are underlined (which is the same as italicizing in word processing software). "Quick" or shorter works, such as articles, poems, and song and episode titles, take quotation marks.

- **Chunking or clustering information.** Combine words or numbers in small groups rather than trying to remember large lists. For example, phone numbers are broken into manageable three- and four-digit chunks (555-5555).

TUTOR TOOLBOX

Here are some popular acrostics:

- **E**very **G**ood **B**oy **D**oes **F**ine: The order of the treble clef lines, low to high (E, G, B, D, F)

- **N**ever **E**at **S**hredded **W**heat: Clockwise compass directions (North, East, South, West)

- **I** **P**eed on the **MAT**: The stages of mitosis (interphase, prophase, metaphase, anaphase, telophase)

- **K**ing **H**enry's **D**irty **U**nderwear **D**oes **C**ontain **M**old: The metric system's prefixes, large to small (kilo-, hecto-, deka-, [base unit of measurement, such as "meter" or "liter"], deci-, centi-, milli-)

- **Method of loci.** To create a visual recollection of items in a list, create in your mind a scenario in which you walk around a familiar room, picking up each item.

- **Music.** In seventh grade, I learned the *Schoolhouse Rock* "Preamble" song. Today, I still sing "We the People" in my head when I want to recollect the contents of this part of the Constitution. (No so with our less-melodic fifth-grade rap about states and capitals, though I do recall that "snow" rhymed with "Juneau.") If no pre-made song exists for your child's current studies, he can set information to his own made-up tune or another favorite song. After all, it worked for the ABCs.

- **Narrative chaining.** Come up with a short, silly story to link items to memorize.

- **Physical tricks.** Make a fist. Now look at your knuckles. Assuming you are in possession of a complete hand, you should have four knuckle peaks and three valleys between them. If you want to figure out how many days are in any given month, count from left to right, starting with January, using both peaks and valleys. Peaks represent thirty-one days, valleys thirty (with the exception of February, whose valley is worth twenty-eight). When you get to July, which is the far-right peak, start again on the left. Some physical tricks combine song and repetition. The song "Heads, Shoulders, Knees, and Toes," is another physical memory trick for younger children (and good exercise).

- **Rhyme.** If memorization makes you feel worse, then put all the words into rhyming verse. For example, the classic rhyme "In fourteen hundred ninety-two, Columbus sailed the ocean blue" reminds students of the year America was "discovered." And there's also the popular spelling trick "I before E except after C, or when sounding like A, as in neighbor and weigh." (For bonus points, add the sentence containing the most common violations of the rule: "Neither the weird financier nor the foreigner seizes leisure at its height.")

- **Visual**. Sometimes it's best to associate a memorization trick with the way the item looks. You may remember that ">" means "greater than" and "<" means "less than," but it may help your child to picture the symbols as mouths that want to eat the larger numbers.

- **Vocabulary tricks.** Mnemonic devices can even be used to help your child remember the spelling and definitions of vocabulary words. Here are some examples:

    grey: The word is spelled with an "E" in *E*ngland.

    gray: The word is spelled with an "A" in *A*merica.

    stationery: It is spelled with "E" for pap*e*r.

    stationary: It is spelled with "A" for st*a*y.

    their: The consonants "own" the vowels, which are trapped inside *th__r*, serving as a reminder that *their* is possessive.

    there: This word contains *here*, serving as a reminder that *there* refers to a location.

    they're: You can almost see the original words, serving as a reminder that *they're* is a contraction of *they are*.

"Mnipulating" Mnemonics

You may need to update a mnemonic because the information it represents has become obsolete, as with "My Very Educated Mother Just Served Us Nine Pickles," whose pickles vanished when Pluto was demoted to a dwarf planet. To modernize, you might try "My Very Educated Mother Just Served Us Naan," or, to include Ceres, Pluto, and Eris, "My Very Educated Mother Just Served Us Creepy Pickled Eels."

Another reason to modernize mnemonics is that some may be obsolete because of changing cultural references. A generation or two ago, the trick for remembering taxonomic order (kingdom, phylum, class, order, family, genus, and species) was to look at the first letters of the words in the phrase "King Phillip Collects Old, Faded Green Stamps."

Students no longer know about Green stamps, so now "Kings Play Chess On Fancy Glass Stools."

You can customize mnemonics for your child. My friend Tom still remembers the eighth-grade device he used to remember Moh's scale of mineral hardness: "Tom Goes Crazy for Apples. Oh, Quick! The Cow Died!" (talc, gypsum, calcite, fluorite, apatite, orthoclase feldspar, quartz, topaz, corundum, diamond).

Family Activity

Coming up with mnemonic devices makes a good family activity to discuss over dinner or on the go. You can ask a child, "Is there anything you're learning now that you wish you had a trick to remember?"

Then engage a child's siblings, parents, grandparents, and friends: "Who can think of a mnemonic to help Gabe remember [the meaning of 'pulchritudinous' / the year World War II started / the order of Earth's atmospheric layers]?"

You can also ask your own questions so your child can practice coming up with mnemonics (and can learn new material in the process). "I wish I could come up with a way to remember the Latin American countries from north to south," you could say, and see what happens.

WHEN LESS IS MORE

Creativity does not have to mean bright lights, sirens, and toys that beep and spin. Creative tutoring can also mean approaching the way you think about education from a new angle. So here's one to consider: in education, less can be more.

Silence

One night, in a crowded sushi restaurant in New York's Greenwich Village, I was introduced to Ryoko, a woman who had recently moved to the United States from Japan. She was teaching Japanese culture to students in Brooklyn, I managed to gather over the surrounding din. Later, near honking cars and street noise, we stood on a sidewalk and I grabbed a few more moments to talk with Ryoko. I needed to get to the essence quickly, as it was hard to hear her. "What would you say is the most important lesson that students could learn from Japanese culture—if you had to teach just one concept?" I asked.

"The importance of silence," she said.[4]

Ryoko's comment seemed ironic, given our surroundings, but she made a good point. I was reminded of "meeting for worship," a tradition in the Quaker community. In the Upper School at Sidwell Friends School, the entire ninth through twelfth grades gather for one class period a week to sit in silence. The students have a chance to reflect on their lives. When moved to speak, individual students can break the silence to share insights.

When we hear chatter surrounded by noise, everything blends together, and little stands out. But in the midst of silence, we start to differentiate. We can focus. Each new element that we do hear takes on a new value.

Boredom

When my colleague Anne Charny moved with her family to Cambodia in 1997, there were fewer opportunities for her children to amuse themselves than they'd been used to in Cambridge, Massachusetts. At first, Anne's children complained that there was nothing to do, and they were right. But after a while, they were forced to invent their own fun, and they started creating and performing their own plays.

TUTOR TOOLBOX

Know how to listen, and you will profit even from those who talk badly.

—Plutarch

That, Anne says, is the "crucial role of boredom." Though it may sound counterintuitive, sometimes lack of external stimulation can provide the impetus that will ignite a child's mind and lead to great creativity.[5]

Simplicity

In plays, significant characters rarely enter for the first time en masse. Rather, they come in one by one—think of them more like gifts at Hanukkah than at Christmas. Ideally, introducing one element at a time gives us the chance to get to know it, to value it independently.

When she was around seven years old, a girl I know received a beautiful bed-and-dresser set for her doll. And, as happens on holidays in homes across the country, she spent the rest of the morning playing with nothing but—you guessed it—the cardboard tube from the inside of the wrapping paper. Sometimes the gifts that inspire creativity the most are the simplest.

My aunt, for example, remembers her father bringing home the gift of a ream of blank paper. It represented endless possibility.

TUTOR TOOLBOX

Fully-scheduled school hours and extracurricular activities leave little time for children to dream, to think, to invent solutions to problems, to cope with stressful experiences, or simply to fulfill the universal need for solitude and privacy.

—Jan Hunt, *The Unschooling Unmanual*

TUTOR TAKE-AWAY

- It pays to think creatively as you foster your child's education.

- Let children teach each other.

- Look for versatile, imagination-building toys.

- Take cues from homeschoolers; for example, help your child create a lapbook.

- Play can be a vital part of your child's "work"—that is, learning.

- Use art and crafts when working with your child.

- Children can, with guidance, combine kinetic movement with study.

- Kids can "play with their food" to learn.

- Mnemonic devices are effective and fun, especially if your family creates their own.

- Consider at-home immersion with educational themes.

- A little deprivation never hurt any student; in fact, it can help.

CHAPTER 5

Put It on the Wall: Living the Parent-Tutor Lifestyle

Astronauts have John Glenn. Brownies have Girl Scouts. Horses have Mr. Ed. But who's an aspiring parent-tutor to admire?

Try Frank and Lillian Gilbreth, the real-life parents of twelve featured in the memoir *Cheaper by the Dozen*, a great read for adults and children alike (not to be confused with the only loosely related Steve Martin film of the same name).

Efficiency expert Frank Gilbreth was always looking for ways to teach, using family picnics to talk about ant colonies, the creation of stone walls by glaciers, and the building of factories. As his children recalled, "If the factory whistle blew, he'd take out his stopwatch and time the difference between when the steam appeared and when we heard the sound."[1] From this, he had the children calculate the speed of sound.

At the dinner table, Gilbreth taught his children to multiply two-digit numbers in their heads. Even their preschooler could mentally multiply two-digit numbers by each other up to twenty-five.

But one of the most noteworthy points about the Gilbreths' lives was how they made use of the space in their home—in particular, their wall space.

Frank Gilbreth taught his children Morse code by painting a key to the code in the bathroom and secret messages on the walls and ceilings of their Nantucket cottage. Some led to prizes. (Though Morse code may no longer be as useful for kids, this technique would still teach the general principles of translation from symbols to words. Or you could try this with a foreign language or mathematical symbols.)

Images in the Gilbreth dining room illustrated the mathematical relationships between meters and feet. Graph paper that measured one thousand squares by one thousand squares provided a visual aid for the concept of a million.

To teach astronomy, Gilbreth painted planets on the walls, to scale, "ranging from little Mercury, represented by a circle about as big as a marble, to Jupiter, as big as a basketball."[2] He hung pictures of stars, nebulae, and solar eclipses—not at adult eye level, but near the floor so that the little children could see the photos as well.

Of course, even Gilbreth—despite being a professional efficiency expert—did not do everything in this chapter. Nor should he have. Gilbreth thought about and put into practice the resources that worked best for his family's home. I invite you to do the same.

EXTREME MAKEOVER: HOME TUTOR EDITION

Houses are filled with blank areas primed (literally) for education: walls, doors, and ceilings. Read biographies and you may notice that famous figures found inspiration in what their parents let them put on household surfaces. As a ten-year-old growing up during the Spanish Civil War, Che Guevara had maps of Spain with flags that marked key locations on the revolutionary front. Remember how Abe Lincoln wrote with charcoal on a shovel? That wasn't all he wrote on. Lincoln also used the charcoal to practice math on his home's walls and doorposts.

Let's review your home room by room, thinking about how to maximize the potential of each room and turn each separately—and all collectively—into an educational powerhouse.

The Kitchen

My college friend Anthony could recall the Supreme Court justices easily, by name and sight. One day I told him I wished that I, too, had gone to a school that emphasized the justices. No, he said, he had learned about the justices at home. Had his parents taught him? Yes, but not in the way I'd thought. Anthony's parents had put a picture of the justices on the refrigerator one day. They didn't discuss the picture, but every time Anthony and his sister went to the kitchen, they couldn't help but see the Supreme Court justices. As a result, they knew them all.

A fridge is a wonderful tabula rasa where you can post whatever you want your child to notice. The presidents. The Chinese zodiac. The anatomy of a swordfish (which I suppose could also go *in* the fridge). Whatever your academic fancy, put it on the fridge.

Create your own magnet school. Besides being a surface for images and articles of note, consider your fridge's other inherent power: magnetism. Choose your magnets wisely. Fine, put up those wedding save-the-dates and the freebies from your dentist and contact lens company. But also save space for the brain-building magnets.

(Once you have magnets, they can also be used on other metal surfaces, including the dishwasher, filing cabinets, and stand-alone magnetic boards.)

- **Magnetic basics.** Letters. Numbers. Sight words. Themed words. Your child can use these readily available categories of magnets to write her name, record a friend's phone number, or leave a secret message for a sibling or parent to see the next time he or she opens the fridge.

- **Foreign language magnets.** Reversible magnets feature a foreign word on one side and the English translation on the other. They're available in Spanish, French, Chinese, German, Italian, Yiddish, Hebrew—even American Sign Language! You can also find raised Braille alphabet magnets.

- **Magnetic grocery lists.** You can ask children learning to read to sort through a collection of grocery-themed magnets to find the foods you need. Write on blank magnets for foods that aren't included in your set. Nonmagnetic lists are also a great way to get beginning writers to practice. Ask your child to add items to the grocery list; this works particularly well when they're items he likes to eat!

- **Magnetic puppet theater.** From Sappho to Emily Dickinson and Fyodor Dostoevsky to Salvador Dali, you can find magnetic finger puppets appropriate for students of any age. Finger puppets can also provide levity on car trips and during history exam prep.

- **Magnetic art.** You can find magnetic art at museum gift shops. If your child admires an artist's work, a magnet can be a good reminder of that artist's name and composition style, as well as the piece itself.

The Dining Room

By "dining room," I'm referring to "dining table" or wherever your children eat, whether in the kitchen or at a coffee table. Ideally, this location doubles as a place for your family to gather and discuss the day. But whether your child eats alone or with others, here's a way to add some educational spice to your table settings.

Placemats. Do your children ever read while they eat? If they're tired of the backs of cereal boxes and already making good use of the newspaper, you can buy or make your own placemats, handy for students of any age.

Placemats for purchase in stores and online include country, continent, and world maps; math facts; print and cursive guides; Roman numerals; foreign words; flags, money, animals, metric conversions, anatomy, telling time, and dinosaurs. But placemats aren't just for little kids. You can find a placemat of the periodic table of the elements for high school students. Constellations or planetary science placemats are available for astronomy students, as are presidential placemats for American history or government information.

You or your children can also make your own placemats. Use paper for the inside and self-adhesive laminating sheets for the outside. Vary your placemats. Children can design placemats to include review material for school. If you're taking a family trip to Florida later in the month, ask your child to design a placemat with a map of Florida or the route that you'll be taking from home. Then everyone has a visual guide to consult as you discuss the trip during meals.

Or just use nonlaminated paper and phase the placemats out as they get dirty. You can deliberately use paper placemats if you'd like your children to write on them. Give children the task of creating family quizzes about their favorite animals or subjects (academic or nonacademic), to be completed during meals. Serve dinner with forks, knives, spoons, and pencils!

The Living Room

If students see tutoring centers, schools, and libraries full of reading matter—and a home devoid of it—it sends the message that reading is for academic environments alone, that its relevance ends upon graduation, making it something to be endured and surmounted, not a feature of everyday adult life. Even if you don't read much yourself, try to signal to your child that yours is a home that values reading as an organic, lifelong activity, not just as a school skill.

How do you do this?

Give reading matter a prominent position in both public and private areas of your household. Place basics so that they are accessible to all family members and guests, preferably in a common area, such as your living room. Include a dictionary. Add foreign language dictionaries and any other frequently used reference books, such as an atlas, almanac, or one-volume encyclopedia.

If you get a newspaper at home, keep it out throughout the day. Leave magazines visible on the coffee table. If you're anticlutter, keep in mind that there really is something more enticing about reading material that sits out, rather than in a magazine holder under the table, forgotten.

The Bedroom

Thanks to Facebook, we're accustomed to posting on our own virtual walls. I think every child should have creative access to a *real* wall. This surface provides a creative outlet and a visual reminder of the child's creativity.

Creative walls. Before you panic—"I'm supposed to let them do *what?*"— here are a few ideas to help you feel good about defacing the house. Consider one or more of these options, depending on your child, the amount of space you have, and the level of wall design permanence you want:

- **Paint a frame.** Designate an area in which it's okay for your child to draw or paint on the wall. With the help of painter's tape, paint a border around the decoration-friendly area. Your child can still be creative, but within a controlled, neatly bounded region. (You may want to keep the painter's tape on while your child is painting, in case she goes over the lines.)

- **Chalkboard paint.** Paint an entire wall or a designated area with chalkboard paint. If you haven't seen it, this paint turns a regular wall into a chalkboard. It can be tinted to create colored

Anybody out there who is a parent, if your kids want to paint their bedrooms, as a favor to me, let them do it. It'll be OK. Don't worry about resale value on the house.

—Randy Pausch, *The Last Lecture*

chalkboard surfaces. It's perfect for a bedroom—also for a family to-do list or an all-purpose message board. (If you prefer, look for whiteboards or peel-and-stick dry erase surfaces.)

- **Magnetic paint.** Similar to the chalkboard paint, this paint turns any wall into a magnetized surface. (See "The Kitchen," page 94, for ideas about what to do with magnets.)

- **Glow-in-the-dark or black-light paint.** The Blue Man Group started the Blue School, a private elementary school in New York City. During "glow time," they turn on the black lights to illuminate paint, shaving cream, and other glowing playthings.

- **Bulletin board.** The traditional cork board works well if you want a surface where you can tack artwork, articles, or other papers of note.

- **Canvas or easel.** For the art gallery look (or if you're nervous about letting a child use art supplies directly on the wall), provide a canvas or standing easel from an art supply store. You can hang, remove, and replace these as needed. For an even less expensive option, try poster board or the side of a large cardboard box.

Bedtime books. Create and maintain a bedtime reading routine. Your child brushes his teeth, gets into pajamas, and then reads with you. It's the last thing you do before your child goes to sleep, creating a soothing routine for your child, who will associate relaxing before bed with reading.

You read to your child. Your child reads to you. You both listen while another child reads. You alternate reading with singing lullabies.

Try to make reading into something exciting, a privilege, a special activity the grownups stay up to do. I wanted to stay up late and lie in my parents' bed to read because I knew it was part of their evening routine. I never begged to stay up watching television because that wasn't what adults did. (It turned out my parents watched TV after I went to sleep.)

This is a good opportunity to use reverse psychology. (See "Reverse Psychology," pages 62–63.)

YOU: I'm not sure if you should stay up to read any longer. It's bedtime.

YOUR CHILD: Please?

YOU: Your brother's already asleep.

YOUR CHILD: He's younger.

YOU: True. Well, then maybe with a flashlight, because you're older.

(See "Keep Reading Aloud," pages 164–66, for more information about reading aloud with older children.)

The Bathroom

It doesn't take a whiz to implement lavatory learning and—though it may sound "loo-ny"—even the drabbest water closet can make your

---

TUTOR TOOLBOX

Flashlights can add to the mystique of solo reading before bed, especially if your child likes camping or associates flashlights with special, secret activities. You can build excitement by making the flashlight a privilege of age: "When you turn eight, you'll be allowed to use a flashlight to read under the covers!"

child privy to a fount of knowledge! Show your child that learning is, well, Number One.

Bath books. While waterproof bath books are traditionally for babies, older students can find waterproof notebooks and pens. Of course, bath-takers willing to risk their books can read anything in the tub. There are a few waterproof books for higher-level readers, but to find copies of classics like *Great Expectations*, you'll have to laminate them yourself. ("You should be grateful to them what laminated you by hand!" you can say, if you've read far enough to make witty *Great Expectations*–based jokes.)

Bath crayons. Kids with special bath crayons (*not* the same as regular wax crayons) can write on both tub and tile. They're perfect for bath-time letter and number practice for *any* age. Older children can use bath crayons during showers to leave messages for siblings, write out spelling words or vocabulary definitions, or review math. Nothing says, "Good morning!" like a noseful of Irish Spring and an eyeful of the quadratic equation.

Bath instruments. These are intended for younger children but fun for all ages, judging from the reviews written by parents who use these themselves. For the aspiring musician, look up water flutes, drums, xylophones, trumpets, and whistles. Presumably they could also be played with as summer water toys or at any time that nearby liquid makes waterproof instruments preferable.

Language lessons. Knowing how much time their children spent near, on, or in the sink, toilet, and bath, the Gilbreths put a Victrola in each of the two bathrooms their children used. It's a move that seems to have been copied by the restaurant chain Olive Garden, which plays Italian language lessons in its restrooms. If you're so inspired, you too can use the bathroom for language lessons.

Posters. If you have the space to hang a framed or laminated poster that's visible from the toilet, your child will have no choice but to see it on occasion. Consider health- or water-themed information. Start early and your child will be an expert in the subject of your choosing by high school graduation—after all, where else can you be absolutely sure your child will have time to sit and read?

Shower curtains. For a more permanent option than bath crayons, try an educational shower curtain. Thanks to the free market, it's possible to shower behind a waterproof sheet featuring foreign vocabulary, SAT words, math facts, a map of the world, or the periodic table of elements.

Inside and Outside

Here, we'll look at home modifications that aren't room-specific. A couple of these ideas are better suited to the great outdoors, namely backyards and driveways (though you can still find ways to use these ideas if you're yard- and driveway-less).

Foreign language labels. These removable stickers allow you to temporarily label items throughout your house. You can also make your own labels using sticky notes.

Picture study. As part of her late-nineteenth-century educational practice, British teacher Charlotte Mason came up with the concept of picture studies. To apply a basic version of her art appreciation approach, each week you can select a famous painting, photograph, or other noteworthy image. Display it somewhere in your home, preferably where it will be visible for a long time—like in the dining room or the back of the driver's seat in the car—and then initiate increasingly complex discussions about the picture over the course of the week. Start on Monday by asking "What do you see?" and progress through the week to "What does it remind you of?" and "What might this tree symbolize?"

The wall of worthies. Though some of Thomas Jefferson's parenting choices may have been suspect (e.g., allegedly keeping some of his own children bound to his land as slaves), he did have at least one clearly admirable parent-tutor quality: he made good educational use of wall space. Most notably, he had what the Monticello guides refer to as his "wall of worthies." Several sides of a sitting room featured twenty-four portraits of the figures Jefferson admired, including the thinkers John Locke, Isaac Newton, and Francis Bacon; explorers Christopher

Columbus and Ferdinand Magellan; and contemporaries George Washington, Benjamin Franklin, and James Madison.

Now this was inspired parenting. How clever to surround yourself and your family with images of notable and inspirational public figures. I wish I'd been encouraged to do this as a child. Some students are inclined to post pictures without prompting, but so often the images on the wall end up being pop icons idolized for superficial qualities—good in moderation, but better if augmented by figures of deeper substance. How much wall space does your child devote to role models? I'd venture to say that images of the *Twilight* actors trump Gandhi at least nine times out of ten on the average American teen's "wall of worthies," even though (with no offense intended to *Twilight* actors) I tend to doubt Kristen Stewart or Robert Pattinson ever did anything so heroic as protesting an unjust tax with a twenty-day Salt Satyagraha to the sea.

I'm not suggesting that children should turn their rooms into shrines to dead, white European men, à la Jefferson. Just that, as you or your child learn about notable people—whether public, private, American, or foreign—you should think about devoting a little bit of your physical space to those people who truly inspire you. Maybe you want your child to take note of our first female secretary of state, Madeline Albright, or our second, Condoleezza Rice. Perhaps you've noticed an article about Kenyan environmentalist and Nobel Peace Prize–winner Wangari Maathai. (For recommendations of periodicals that might feature worthwhile articles or profiles to discuss with your kids, see the Resources section, page 184.) Maybe you want to feature family members who are admirable, especially pictured in their work environments. Create your own wall (or hallway, fridge, bulletin board, etc.) of worthies.

The yard and driveway. Chalk turns your sidewalk and driveway into a giant slate. Use it for hopscotch, snail, and other math-based games.

You can make your own sidewalk paint with this simple recipe: one part cornstarch plus one part water plus a little food coloring. (Incidentally, for those of you who have read *Bartholomew and the Oobleck*, Dr. Seuss's Oobleck is two parts cornstarch plus one part water plus green food coloring. Technically, Oobleck is a "non-Newtonian fluid." Less technically, it's a lot of fun.)

The garden. Whether you have a window box or dirt plot, plant a garden. Your child can learn about herbs, vegetables, and flowers. If you have an adult-sized plot, give your child her own smaller area to plant and harvest. Combine gardening with science: chart multiple plants' growth when treated differently—for example, when watered with different substances, fertilized versus unfertilized, or exposed to varied amounts of sun.

WHAT YOUR HOUSE SAYS ABOUT YOU

Think about what message the rooms in your house send—and what messages they *could* send.

Imagine you and your spouse or partner disappeared right now. Now imagine your children had to grow up in your home without you there. Based purely on the visual clues in the home, how would your children think you wanted them to spend their time?

Thinking along the same lines, consider these questions:

- What objects are the focal points of each of the rooms in your home? Do you feature the computer? Bookshelves? A TV? A piano?

- Which room is the center of your home, and how do you use it?

- If you subscribe to a newspaper, do you leave it where everyone can see it, or does a parent take it to work and leave it there? Or do you clip the coupons, save the TV listings, and immediately recycle the rest?

- What's bigger, your DVD collection or your book collection, and why?

- How many of your rooms contain reading matter?

- Do you have more things that say "hands off" than "hands on"?

- If you have a family computer, what is its homepage when you open a browser? Google? A newspaper? NYTimes.com? CNN.com?

Though some of these may sound like leading questions, there aren't right or wrong answers to them. I just want to make you aware of the messages that your home and its contents send to your children and to make sure that you have considered and actively approve of these messages.

Consider What You Compartmentalize

Do you keep writing implements in each room of your house, and can your child reach them? Easily accessible pens, pencils, crayons, and paper send the message that someone in your home might have something worthwhile to write or draw at a moment's notice. If you're a family that keeps pens in only one place—on the desk in the office, for example—it signals that writing is something compartmentalized, like toilet paper, which can only be used in certain places, as opposed to an omnipresent, multipurpose tool.

The Library

What's that? The library's not part of your home? Well, guess what: it should be. Think of the library as an extension of your house and your local librarian as a relative (albeit a quiet one) in your extended family. He should be able to recommend books to you and, ideally, know your child by name.

Book Smarts: A Library Quiz for Parent-Tutors

I asked one of my teenage students whether she had a bookstore or library near her house, and she had no idea. Would your child know?

Take this quiz and then educate your child about libraries:

1. Does your child have a library card?

2. Has she been to the local public library?

3. Has she been to more than one local library?

4. If yes to (3), can your child differentiate between local libraries (e.g., one has better foreign language materials and the other has a great young adult's section)?

5. Does your family—and your child—know at least one librarian by name? Does at least one librarian know your child by name? (If not, have you ever introduced your child to the librarian?)

6. Does your child know she can ask librarians for book recommendations?

7. Has your child ever done this or seen you doing this?

8. Can your child find books that she has enjoyed? Can she name them?

9. Can your child find books by authors she enjoys?

10. Can your child find books in genres she enjoys (e.g., science fiction, travel, or poetry)?

11. Can your child find books about subjects she enjoys (e.g., baseball, animal care, or baking)?

Ways the Library Beats Amazon

- The library is cheaper—free, in fact.
- Borrowing books is better for the planet. You'll be saving manufacturing, transportation, and environmental resources.

- There's no obligation. No one needs to feel guilty about not reading a full library book. There's no harm in stopping a few pages into a book if it's not a good fit for the reader, so trying new authors and genres is not a risk. (I once overheard a young child at a bookstore ask her mother, concerned, "But what if I don't want to keep it?" Her mother replied, "That's not how it works here." Kids don't always want to feel tied to a book they may not enjoy.)

- You can read books there.

- Libraries have lectures, story times, summer reading programs, and even library sleepovers.

- Kids can also see you browsing, trying materials, and getting a taste of new subjects that you might not pay to invest in but are curious about. As a result, they may develop a wider range of interests.

- The library creates an element of tension and an impetus to read. When your child checks a book out of the library, you can explain that you *only* have this book for X more days, so he'll need to finish reading it soon.

Keep library books in a specific place in your home so that your child encounters other family members' books regularly, especially when getting ready to go to or from the library or checking due dates. Stop at the library as an errand, and let your child see that checking out books is as routine as going to the supermarket or the bank.

Notebooks

Does your child own a notebook? I'm not talking about school notebooks, composition notebooks filled with vocabulary words, spiral-bound notebooks that you keep on a shelf, or telephone pads on tables that everyone in the family accesses freely. I want to know whether your child has at least one personal notebook, one that is his *alone*, cover to cover. Has he ever had one?

On the whole, American parents are good about making sure their children have access to books; personal notebooks, not as much.

Your child should have a place where he can write, draw, or record anything. Let him pick the notebook size and style. When I was six or seven, I liked using a spiral-bound, multisubject notebook with thick lines. It made me feel grownup, important, and like Harriet the Spy. Now, I use 3.5"x 5.5" pocket-sized notebooks with an elastic band that holds the front closed and a string that marks my current page. I like that they fit in my pocket, the string lets me open directly to my page without flipping through my notes in front of people, and the pages are small enough to let me move through quickly and feel a sense of satisfaction as I move forward to a new notebook. Clearly, the feelings of privacy and productivity mean a lot more to me now than they did when I was younger.

Do not regulate how your child uses his notebook. Do not pry. It is fine for children of any age to have a private notebook. You can suggest uses—but don't turn having a notebook into work. Just as kids have fun reading books in which they don't have to look up every word they don't know, they should have an unregulated notebook that's a safe place for them to write or draw or do whatever they want. Your level of involvement in these will vary depending on the age of your child, but all types of journals are appropriate for kids from K–12:

- **Daily journal.** Forcing a daily journal can be a grind. If you want to get your child into the habit of writing daily, maybe come up with a limited goal. For example: Write down your favorite moment from today. What would you want to remember? Did you meet someone new? Did you hear a funny quote? Did you accomplish anything? What would you like to do again? What do you wonder about? What did you do today that made you feel proud?

- **Book, magazine article, movie, television show, radio program, story, public speaker journals.** Your child can write what is most memorable about any of these that they experienced. Would you recommend this movie? If so, to whom? What were the speaker's key points? What message was the show trying to communicate? Did it work? What would you want to remember if you looked back at this journal in ten years?

- **Be like Oprah and have a gratitude journal.** I'm not sure whether it helps with gratitude, but writing down what he's grateful for definitely gets your child thinking.

Journals are valuable not just for in-the-moment writing practice and reflection. Kids will also appreciate looking back at them to see how they've grown as writers and as people. With only ten minutes of writing a night, imagine the archives your child will have. If possible, make journal writing into a regular, routine event, much like a bedtime story.

Learning as a Matter of Course

Good parent-tutors use maps to make sure their children can identify countries that come up in conversation. They carry books for themselves and their kids in case of waits at the doctor or dentist. They ask their children questions and they listen—*really* listen—to the answers, every single day.

The parent-tutor household is not a pressure cooker in which parents and children are primarily motivated by name-brand schools or clothes, or by fame and fortune. Rather, these households support learning because they believe it is important in and of itself to be educated human beings. You, too, can adopt their simple and rewarding philosophy: Why do we learn? Because learning is something our family values. Learning is what we do.

TUTOR TAKE-AWAY

- Use the space in your home to help educate your children.

- The Gilbreths, of *Cheaper By the Dozen* fame, provide inspiring and practical ideas for parent-tutors.

- Every room in your house can provide learning opportunities; for instance, young children in the kitchen will appreciate going to a "magnet school" on the refrigerator.

- Teenagers have a virtual wall online—give all kids a real one.

- The big three of "putting it on the wall": a world map, a place to draw or innovate, and something your child has created.

- Consider what your house says about your values.

- The public library should be an extension of your home.

- Children benefit from owning a personal notebook—with no parental snooping allowed!

- The parent-tutor household supports learning for its own sake.

iDon't Think iKnow Where My Homework Is: Helping Kids Connect and Organize for the Twenty-First Century

My students text, Tweet, Skype, blog, Yelp, YouTube, podcast, IM, Google, and Facebook, filling their days with action verbs that, as recently as the turn of the millennium, were largely unknown (or reserved for animals). For parents still figuring out how to convert Betamax and LaserDiscs to a usable format, it can be hard to keep up. It may even seem like technology has become ungovernable. After all, as the 2010 Kaiser Family Foundation survey "Generation M: Media in the Lives of 8- to 18-Year-Olds" found, the average child uses recreational* electronic media for seven hours and thirty-eight minutes *each*

---

* In other words, nonacademic. These numbers *do not* include the time students spend using electronic media for schoolwork.

day.[1] In *addition*, the group found that the average seventh to twelfth grader spends one hour and thirty-five minutes each day sending and receiving text messages and thirty-three minutes talking on the phone. Just to be clear, these numbers mean that more than one-third of a child's waking life (or one entire year out of every three) is spent in front of electronic media.

If your reaction to those statistics is to turn off, tune out, and drop (the electronics) in the recycling bin, I won't stop you. But there is a middle ground. When you power up your gadgets, you can empower yourself at the same time. It's part of the job—and fun—of being your child's tutor to learn how to make technology work *for* you rather than against you.

MAKING THE MOST OF TWENTY-FIRST-CENTURY TECHNOLOGY

Before going into some of the specifics of what the world of technology has to offer, I have one caveat: younger children using these technologies should be supervised, much as they would be if they were watching TV or movies. It's tempting to let electronic devices distract your child for a few hours and give you a parental breather, and it is in fact possible to do so responsibly—*if* you screen or otherwise approve the material first.

That said, here's an A-to-Z (A-to-Y, actually) sampler of what the twenty-first century has to offer. Hopefully some of the examples in this chapter will inspire you to come up with ways to use technology to enrich your child's education. For more information about student-friendly software, websites, and other interactive media, you can subscribe to magazines such as *Children's Technology Review* (childrenstech.com), read news and reviews from Edutaining Kids (edutainingkids.com), or consult the thousands of reviews that parents and educators have posted on Common Sense Media (commonsensemedia.org), which you can also follow on Facebook and Twitter.

Audio Books

Before literature was written, it was transmitted orally. You and your child can travel back to that magical age of storytelling through the audio book. Recordings ranging from nursery rhymes to novels can entertain the whole family on long car rides (though you can also choose a family member to read aloud). On a practical level, for the avid reader, this technology lets you give your eyes a rest while still "reading."

I worked with a kindergarten student who loved to hear stories that were well beyond his reading level. When his parents were busy, they provided him with wonderful audio books, and he would curl up with a blanket under the dining table and listen.

Students can supplement or review their in-class reading with audio books. Some volumes of Shakespeare's plays now come with CDs of actors reading the scenes, which can help make challenging material more engaging.

Audio books are available in the library and from online sources, including Apple (iTunes), Amazon, and Audible. Other free audio-book sources include the websites Librivox and Lit2Go.

Several language-learning programs are audio-based, which makes sense because language is largely about listening and speaking. Such programs can supplement a student's in-class language learning, provide an introduction to a language the summer before beginning formal study, teach a language to a student who can't study it in school, or help you learn a new language as a whole family. My personal favorite among language-learning programs is Pimsleur; it has lessons that engage students in conversation rather than just having them memorize lists of foreign words.

TUTOR TOOLBOX

Calculators can be a useful tool to facilitate math work, but please do stop your child from grabbing a calculator for problems that could be done mentally or easily solved on paper.

For audio lectures on academic subjects, have your middle or high school student try *The Great Courses* (http://www.teach12.com/great courses.aspx?ai=16281), a series that offers subjects ranging from "Understanding the Universe" to "Calculus Made Clear" to "The American Civil War" to "From Yao to Mao: 5000 Years of Chinese History."

Blogs

Some students create their own blogs, which can be great writing practice and even inspire readers to leave comments, engaging the blogger in a written dialogue. Blog posts should be carefully monitored, since what your child writes in this diary-like format is broadcast to the world and will be cached by services such as Google, meaning deleting a post won't necessarily remove it from the Web. There may be age restrictions for blog use, depending on the service you use. You can encourage your child to use a pseudonym (such as a fun nickname) when blogging (and elsewhere online) and remind him not to reveal sensitive or identifying information.

Cell Phones

Cell phones that don't have access to the Internet generally have little to offer in terms of education besides tip calculators, and I don't believe in using those, as almost everyone should be able to calculate a tip of 10, 15, or 20 percent.*

If your child has what is generally referred to as a *smartphone*, she can use it as a learning tool; smartphones allow users to access a gigantic portion of accumulated human knowledge within seconds. On a whim, a student can find facts, sources, and arguments about a subject that she

---

* Food costs $28.00? Move the decimal place to the left to find 10 percent: $2.80. If you want to leave 20 percent, double it: $5.60. If you want to leave 15 percent, find 5 percent (half of $2.80) and add it to the original 10 percent ($2.80): $2.80 + $1.40 = $4.20. Want to leave closer to 18 percent? Just leave an amount between $4.20 and $5.60. You will not need a cell phone tip calculator if you can do this.

might have otherwise ignored. Want to know the capital of Tanzania? It's Dar es Salaam. What time is sunset in Anchorage in mid-August? It's at 10 p.m. How do lightning rods work? (That one's too complicated to answer here. Look it up on your smartphone.)

As of this writing, free or minimally expensive (under $5) educational apps (software applications) for the iOS platform (Apple's iPhone, iPad, and iPod Touch) include reference-based tools such as dictionaries (dictionary.com), encyclopedias (Wikipedia Mobile), e-readers with free e-book access (MegaReader), geography games (U.S. Geography by Discovery Education), grammar quizzes (Grammar App), language translators (Free Translator), and the US constitution (Constitution). There are math and science apps, including formula finders (iFormulas), the periodic table (Periodic Table of the Elements), scientific term lists (Science Glossary), and unit conversion calculators (Convert—the unit calculator). Organizational and study skills tools exist for flashcard creation (Flashcards Deluxe) and homework organization (iHomework and myHomework). Astronomers can identify stars, planets, and constellations simply by pointing a smartphone at the sky (Google Sky Map and Virtual Sky Astronomy). For young students, there are apps with geography puzzles (United States Puzzle Map) and even live zoo cameras (Pocket Zoo). Many of these applications (with slightly different names or different publishers) are also available on other smartphone platforms, such as Android and WebOS.

Smartphones can also provide distractions in the form of games, videos, and web browsing, and—as always—some amount of oversight is important.

Classes Online

With the modern-day equivalent of correspondence classes, students of all ages can learn from online video lectures available through companies such as Thinkwell. Homeschoolers take these classes year round; nonhomeschoolers can choose to take advantage of the self-paced classes over summer breaks.

Your high school student can also take advantage of online college classes, giving him a head start on determining what field of study he might enjoy. For example, one of Harvard University's most popular classes, *Justice*, taught by Professor Michael Sandel, has video lectures available for free on its own website, along with a collection of discussion guides filled with thought-provoking moral quandaries: "Suppose ten thousand innocent civilians live next to a munitions factory in a country at war. If you bomb the factory, all of them will die. If you don't bomb the factory, it will be used to produce bombs that will be dropped on fifty thousand innocent civilians in another country. What's the right thing to do?"[2]

Also check out MIT OpenCourseWare, which provides free access to most of the Massachusetts Institute of Technology's undergraduate- and graduate-level lectures and coursework. Classes range from "Archery" to "Women in South Asia" to (here's a new one to worry about, parents) "Nuclear Reactor Safety."

Digital Cameras

As students learn to take high-quality, smartly composed photographs, they can use these pictures for photo contests, photo essays, and captioned photo albums.

Sites like Flickr allow photo posters to attract a group of online acquaintances who provide photo critiques—a source of constructive feedback that might otherwise only be available in a photography class. Students can use Flickr's world map to browse pictures based on where they were taken and in the process build geographical awareness, knowledge of travel and culture (often aided by captions), and, of course, a sense of photographic artistry.

As a parent-tutor, you can be the photographer who facilitates a creative project or personal storytelling exercise. During a tutoring session, I took pictures as a young student used a detective costume, jewelry, and his pet rabbit to act out a story he'd made up: "The Fuzzy Thief." We then uploaded the photos into a Word document, discussing dramatic story progression. From there, he wrote a dialogue-rich story to go along with the pictures. At the end of a project like this, you can use book templates provided by an online photo-printing service such as MyPublisher to submit the story for printing and binding.

Your child can set up photography shows for his neighborhood or for family get-togethers. He can ask neighbors, family members, and friends to each provide a digital picture that relates to a particular theme—say, Thanksgiving—or has a compelling, scary, or funny story behind it. Your child organizes the pictures and writes up a brief description for each one, in the process learning about people's travels and experiences; practicing the arts of interviewing, listening, taking notes, and writing concise summaries; and putting on an exhibit. If an in-person event is too complicated, arrange a virtual photo display online or print and mail an exhibit brochure.

DVRs

Digital video recorders, TiVo among them, can automatically tape a whole series or season of a show and save them in a list for easy viewing. You can preselect and save shows that would be beneficial to your child and allow her to watch them at leisure in lieu of flipping through channels. With the touch of a button or two, my husband and I taped a *Planet Earth* marathon and later played it repeatedly for a young visitor, who was enthralled by the fish.

eBay

Use eBay to teach children about the business of sales: rip-offs, sneaky advertising, the psychological effect of sale deadlines, and the occasional good deal.

E-books and E-readers

In 2009, the Massachusetts boarding school Cushing Academy renovated and, in the process, replaced their twenty-thousand-volume library with hundreds of thousands of web-based books available to their (as of 2010) approximately two hundred e-readers.

As Cushing Academy foresaw and technological developments seem to indicate, e-reading is here to stay. Bear in mind its academic disadvantages, though: with e-books, it's harder to annotate text, get a tactile sense of how far into a book you've come, flip between passages with ease, or read in the bathtub. On the other hand, e-readers are easy to transport, environmentally friendly, and potentially exciting to use.

If you would like to introduce your child to an e-reader, options include the Kindle, Nook, iPad, and even the Nintendo DS, which now offers a *100 Classic Books* collection. Smartphones such as the iPhone and Android devices support digitally published formats and can hook into the Kindle store. There's also the VTech V.Reader, which has been billed as the first animated, touchscreen e-reader for three- to seven-year-olds.

For free books, try Project Gutenberg, Bartleby, and Google Books. With the "Find in a library" option, Google Books will search globally to identify the closest library that has a physical copy of the book you're reading online. (One book I was interested in turned out to be 8,400 miles from me, in South Africa.) One might also have success by searching Google for the name of the book and including terms such as *PDF, EPUB,* or *e-book*.

Be aware that e-book readers and computers are becoming increasingly important as a cheaper, lighter, greener way to read textbooks. Publishers are experimenting with digital formats that may replace physical textbooks. California has taken the lead on the move toward free digital textbook access, with an abundance of books and other materials available online via the California Learning Resource Network.

E-mail

Take your child to a nice stationery store, have her pick out an appealing, good-quality box of stationery and a pen, and then train her in the art of letter writing. Then encourage her to translate these skills to the e-mail world. Your child will be much more prepared than her "LOL"-ing friends when it comes to corresponding with teachers, college professors, and employers later on.

You can also ask your child to be the family scribe, collecting messages from members of your immediate family to send in a family e-mail to a friend or relative.

Any entrepreneurial student can also create a newsletter (e-mailed or printed) to fill a local niche. Perhaps a neighborhood update with information about animal sightings, plants that grow well in local gardens, where to volunteer, stores with the best school supplies, or the best new movies, books, or restaurants. Your child's siblings, friends, and other local children can get involved and have different reporting beats. Besides the obvious benefits of the endeavor—writing experience— your child will have a greater sense of community. This could also be a project that shows initiative and therefore makes a college application– worthy credential.

Facebook

This social networking site was created by and for Harvard students in 2004. It is now in use by the thirteen-and-older set worldwide. Some schools have tried to discourage the use of Facebook, both to limit screen time and to control cyberbullying. If your child does create a Facebook account, you might consider joining so you can inconspicuously keep tabs on what's going on.

On Facebook, your child can "Like" museums, magazines, newspapers, or performing arts organizations—for example, the American Museum of Natural History. By doing this, she will see updates and article links appearing on the Newsfeed (the main page, which provides recent updates about a member's friends and organizations).

As a parent-tutor and Facebook member, you can join a Facebook group to hear and share educational ideas. Among the groups catering to homeschoolers (and, therefore, applicable to all parents) are "Peace Hill Press," "Home Education Magazine," and "TOS Homeschool Crew."

When using social networking sites besides Facebook, the same basic principles apply: Check for age restrictions. Be familiar with your child's profile and ensure that he understands how to use privacy settings so that his information is restricted to friends. Ask your child for updates about social networking sites regularly, much as you would ask about what's new in his nonvirtual social life.

Computer Games

The field of educational and fun computer software has expanded since
the era of Number Munchers and the Speak & Spell. Today's top-rated
products include software that allows you to view digital images direct
from your USB-connected microscope (Digital Blue: QX5 Computer
Microscope), study music with "Maestro Max" (Music Ace Deluxe), create a simulated zoo (Zoo Tycoon 2), learn fractions while saving Spec-
tacle City (Math Missions), design Rube Goldberg-esque machines to
solve puzzles (Crazy Machines: Wacky Contraptions), and use logic
skills to save little blue jelly-bean-like creatures as they escape from the
evil Bloats (Zoombinis: Logical Journey).

You can also find educational games online. I have seen adults and
children alike hooked on the Sheppard Software site (sheppardsoftware
.com), whose free lessons and games let students test themselves on the
chemical elements, fractions, world geography, and even animal classi-
fication.

Global Positioning System (GPS) Devices

Even though my own GPS device has tried to lead me off a cliff at
least twice, this device has legitimate educational value. Your GPS can
motivate your child to be a modern-day explorer. Travel with a detailed
road atlas. Have your child map out car trip routes in advance. Compare
them to the routes the GPS suggests. Another option: Drive the GPS's

route and see if your child can trace the route on a physical map as you go. Can your child guess the GPS's next step? If you're not in a rush, let your child navigate and see what happens. (The GPS will correct you if you get too lost.) If you use your GPS to locate "attractions" such as food, gas, and parks, see if your child can identify the same hot spots for these attractions by looking at the physical map.

Introduce your child (or whole family) to the hobby of geocaching. Hobbyists worldwide use geographic coordinates to hunt for treasures that other geocachers have hidden. As a scientist from the U.S. Naval Observatory put it, "Geocaching is using GPS—a multibillion dollar government system—to find Tupperware in the woods."[3]

Google Maps and Google Earth

Use Google Maps to locate countries, cities, and streets. If your child reads a passage referencing the extraordinary traffic near Zubovskaya Square, on one of Moscow's ring roads, zoom in on the region in Google Maps. You'll be able to get close enough on the satellite view to ask your child to count the lanes (eighteen!), and you can even drag the little yellow Google man onto the map for a panoramic street view.

Google Earth will "fly" you between locations and has three-dimensional city maps and (free) downloadable three-dimensional tours, including trips to the world's famed bridges, skyscrapers, and castles. If you're helping your child with a science assignment about the size of Australia's Ayers Rock, for example, you can have her fly to ground level at the base of the rock and look up.

Movies

This may sound neo-Puritanical, but I recommend limiting family film viewing to just a handful of valuable, inspirational movies a year. Younger students can watch musicals that transmit historical or cultural messages, such as *West Side Story* (which is also educational in that it's based on *Romeo & Juliet*), *Fiddler on the Roof*, and *The Sound of Music* and adaptations of classic books, such as *The Wizard of Oz*. Older students can watch the stories of powerful agents of change: *Gandhi*, *Malcolm X*, *MILK*, *Schindler's List*. Use historical fiction to motivate an interest in historical figures and time periods: the HBO miniseries *John Adams* and *Rome*. For high-quality documentaries, try films by Ken Burns, acclaimed for *The Civil War* and *Baseball*, among others. Even movies not strictly intended as educational can inspire an appreciation of filmmaking and storytelling, such as Disney's *Fantasia* and Roberto Benigni's *Life Is Beautiful*.

If you want to own DVDs, Blu-Ray discs, or digital downloads (rather than rent or borrow them), here are a few of my recommended selection criteria for choosing films:

1. Selected films should have repeat-viewing or lending value.
2. You would want every member of your family to watch them.
3. You would recommend them to your children's friends and their families.
4. You would want to display the films in your home as conversation pieces.
5. The films are reminders of the traits you'd like your child to acquire or the values of your family.

Remember Baby Einstein? They offered refunds to customers in 2009 after research discredited their claim that baby DVDs were educational. Unless new information emerges, limit your use of video content for children younger than three; studies have not shown television or movies to be worth their while.

TUTOR TOOLBOX

The American Academy of Pediatrics recommends limiting TV, movie, and video and computer game time to one or two hours a day and advises that parents not let children have TVs in their bedrooms.

Netflix

Netflix allows you, very simply, to rent by mail or "watch instantly" a wide range of feature films, television shows, and documentaries. Reading *Great Expectations* at school? Netflix has at least six different versions of the film, with the earliest from 1946 and two available for instant viewing.

You can use the Netflix "Instant Queue" to create a list of films worth your child's time or relevant to your child's upcoming course of study. As with all other online resources, do monitor what your child finds herself. A child searching for films about "guinea pigs" will find the unrated Japanese film *Za ginipiggu 2: Chiniku no hana*, which translates to *Guinea Pig: Flower of Flesh and Blood* and shows a killer slowly dismembering his victim—not your average afterschool special, nor of use to a child interested in learning more about the life and diet of Mr. Piggles.

News Aggregators

A student can keep up with his favorite websites by visiting them one after another, and repeating this process over the course of the day, or he can use an aggregation service such as Google Reader to automatically pull the latest updates from these sites. This technology is generally referred to as *RSS*, or *Really Simple Syndication*.

RSS feeds provide an efficient means of conducting research on current events. Say your child is studying climate change in Western Europe. He could use an RSS reader to cull articles on this topic from *Le Monde*, the BBC World News, and any other sites he specifies. Used effectively, this technology becomes your student's personal research assistant.

Podcasts

Your child can listen to podcasts on the computer, on an MP3 (digital music and/or video) player, or burned onto a CD for use at home, in the car, or elsewhere. Check out WNYC's *RadioLab*, the *New Yorker*'s fiction (and nonfiction) podcasts, *The Classic Tales Podcast*, *Grammar Girl*, *The Math Dude*, and the BBC's *Maths Challenge*. To supplement or take the place of a classroom language course, students can use foreign language podcasts, including *Coffee Break Spanish* and the Peace Corps's online language lessons (including Bambara, Thai, and Ukranian), among many others. Podcasts can be accessed through the Amazon store, on iTunes, on an individual show's website, or via a web or smartphone search.

Radio

You can give your child's language skills a boost with talk radio from around the globe, such as Radio France Internationale for French. Using a media player such as Windows Media Player or iTunes, it's easy to browse foreign stations and news and talk radio stations, among plenty of others. Try National Public Radio, also known as NPR, whose best programs include high-quality news (*Morning Edition* and *All Things Considered*), nonfiction storytelling (*This American Life*), engaging science stories (*Radiolab*), and automotive troubleshooting (*Car Talk*).

If your child is studying a particular era, play music by searching for contemporaneous composers and songwriters or selecting a relevant music genre on the Internet radio service Pandora.

Skype and Other Voice over Internet Protocol (VoIP) Services

Let's say this week is "Magnetohydrodynamics Week" at your child's elementary school. Your child has to draw a diagram of the currents moving in Earth's magnetosphere. Bad news: You know it would take ages for you to figure out how to help your child. Good news: Your mother (your child's grandmother) just happens to be a world-class magnetohydrodynamics current diagram expert. Bad news: Your mother lives across the country, and this project is too complicated for a phone conversation. Good news: Your mother has a web camera and Skype, as do you! This means your child can talk to and see his grandmother for free and, more important (in this case, at least), can look at her drawings. She and your child can show each other images as they speak.

This approach also works well for math problems, for explaining projects and other assignments to a grandparent or to a parent who is away from home, and for the all-around fun of seeing another person while you speak to him or her. Look up "Skype Extras" to find collaborative applications, including a shared whiteboard. Adobe's Acrobat.com offers similar video/audio conferencing features and free whiteboard and file-sharing tools.

Television

There's a litany of reasons to oppose excessive television viewing, but I'll provide just one disturbing statistic reported in 2001 by the American Academy of Pediatrics (AAP): The average seventy-year-old will have watched television for a total of seven to ten *years* of his or her life.[4] (Expand that to include other types of screen time, and the number gets even more frightening.) Just as movies should be viewed only in moderation, it is also worth limiting television time. The AAP recommends removing televisions from children's bedrooms and limiting daily "entertainment media" (movies, online viewing, and computer games included) to one to two hours of "quality programming."

Twitter

This online social networking site, which restricts messages to 140 characters, also restricts membership to those eighteen or older. But because anyone can still search Twitter's feeds (and just can't officially "follow" others or write "tweets"), here's some advice: as on Facebook, you or your child can read about cultural institutions, such as museums. The Royal Shakespeare Company used Twitter to produce *Such Tweet Sorrow*, a tweeted version of *Romeo and Juliet*, which could be an interesting supplement to an academic reading of the play. You can follow tweets allegedly coming from the whale model at New York's Natural History Museum or animal facts tweeted (by the aviary contingent, perhaps) from the Maryland Zoo.

Websites

This is obviously a gigantic category. Guide your children toward Internet sites that focus on learning. Students can make flashcards with Quizlet, hear foreign words pronounced at Forvo, or use EyePlorer to narrow down a broad research topic. At the very least, make sure your child has three high-quality websites bookmarked: a dictionary (such as Merriam-Webster), a search engine (probably Google), and a national news source (try the *New York Times*, National Public Radio, or your local paper).

YouTube

Studying Nelson Mandela? Search for him on YouTube and you'll find a 3.5-minute clip from 1961 of his first-ever television interview; the 1990 BBC interview filmed immediately upon his release from prison; his 1994 presidential inauguration address; and a 6.5-minute *Biography* piece about his life.

Besides individual YouTube videos of historical, cultural, and news value, there are also "channels" that institutions and organizations run. For example, Google has its own YouTube channel on which it posts author talks, and the American Museum of National History uses its YouTube channel to show clips about exhibits.

Webby Awards

Since 1996, the Webby Awards have been giving annual honors to the best of the World Wide Web. Among the categories that can be relevant to home education are "Activism," "Cultural Institutions," "Education," "Family/Parenting," "Radio/Podcasts," "Science," and "Youth." Check out webbyawards.com for current and previous winners.

THE MYTH OF MULTITASKING

Multitasking—supposedly, everybody's doing it. Does it hurt or help us? (Wait—before you read any farther, what was the first word on page 32? If you don't remember, check.) Okay, so, at the very least, we're probably in agreement that adding a second task (going back to another page in a book) slows down the first (reading a paragraph).

Need to explain to your skeptical child that multitasking during homework time is a bad idea? Introduce her to reality.

YOUR CHILD: (*talking, texting, checking a Facebook update, and doing algebra homework*): But I can concentrate on homework and my messages at the same time!

REALITY: No, you can't. According to research conducted by a group of UCLA psychologists in 2006, distracted people process new information in the striatum, which is the part of the brain that handles automatic, familiar information, rather than the hippocampus, which normally handles new information.[5]

YOUR CHILD: Meaning?

REALITY: Meaning focused students end up being able to recall information more easily. It goes into the part of the brain that allows you to pull information back out and apply it to new situations.

YOUR CHILD: And what's happening to the information I'm processing?

REALITY: It's in a part of the brain that's much less flexible, so you'll have trouble using it when you see it in new contexts.

YOUR CHILD: Like on tests?

REALITY: On tests. In class discussions. And anywhere else you see it for the rest of your life.

YOUR CHILD: Ouch.

REALITY: Oh, and remember when I said that David Meyer, a psychologist at the University of Michigan, said that multitasking has a negative effect on short-term memory?[6]

YOUR CHILD: I don't remember that.

REALITY: Exactly. I said it to you earlier when you were multitasking, and you've already forgotten.

YOUR CHILD: Eek.

REALITY: Meyer also showed that people who switch between tasks lose time during the changeover. Imagine if you're driving and texting or talking on a cell phone. What happens if you lose even half a second?

YOUR CHILD: I could hit someone?

REALITY: Exactly.

YOUR CHILD: So what do I do?

REALITY: One task. Ignore everything else until it's done.

Of course, advising a child—or even an adult—not to multitask is like telling a teenager to get 8.5 to 9.5 hours of sleep. It's good advice, and it's important, but realistically it will end up as one factor to consider rather than the basis of an instant lifestyle renovation. But please do encourage your child to consider it.

THE ORGANIZED CHILD

What is organization?

Principle 1

Organization is the practice of putting like with like, forming a hierarchy, and sticking to the rules.

So, when it comes to academic papers, what's a "like"?

- Year
- Subject
- Unit
- Type of assignment (tests and quizzes, notes, homework assignments)
- Date (within any larger group, organize chronologically)

Principle 2

The broader the category, the bigger its storage unit. So, for example, a whole year's worth of material might end up in a storage box, a semester's worth in an accordion file, and one subject's worth in a small binder, with the day's loose papers in a paper folder.

Principle 3

Come up with organizational rules and stick to them. There's not one "right" set of rules. Some schools will mandate a certain method of storing papers. Others won't. You can organize using the categories listed above, using color, number, and alphabetical order as needed. What's key is that your child understand his own system of rules and stick with them, changing only to test out a new system that might improve upon the old.

I'm not saying that all people *need* organizational rules. But almost every single person can benefit from them. Once you have rules, then the answer to a question that students ask themselves daily, for the duration of their educational careers—"Where do I put this?"—will become rote. This can be liberating. It will free your child's mind and provide a clarity that might, without him realizing it, have been lacking.

To train your child to have good habits, begin early. Starting when your child is young, do a daily organization check. Have him open his backpack and show you his papers. How did he decide where to put them? If you have to sign permission slips, show your child that you put them back in a particular part of a folder. When your child finishes homework, make sure he understands where completed work goes. Soon enough, your child should pick up what you're doing and be able to follow suit, without guidance. Start each year the same way, with organizational interaction and prompting as long as needed, until your child can organize papers without you and does so as a matter of routine.

Even academically gifted students can benefit from reviewing their organizational system. For a child who is "successful" in school, teachers sometimes do not consider organization, and a serviceable system never gets replaced by a stellar one. You, as the parent-tutor, can take the time to make sure your child gets individualized organizational help.

TUTOR TOOLBOX

Strive for a place for every paper and every paper in its place.
Or, said another way, each piece of paper needs a designated home.

Computer Files

Digital data, whether on a family or personal computer or a flash drive, should be organized using a similar system to that described above, but with word processing documents and folder icons.

Bookmarked or favorite pages can also be kept in folders by subject or, for a family computer, by family member. As a general rule, on shared computers, try to keep each family member's work in a separate folder or account to minimize virtual clutter on the desktop. Within an account or folder, group computer files by year, subject, and project, labeling drafts so that their chronological order is clear.

My Dog Ate My Flash Drive: Keeping Track of Computer Assignments

If your child completes and turns in assignments electronically, make sure he follows these practices:

- **Regularly saves his or her work.** Does your child know the keyboard shortcut for saving? Do you back up your computer files regularly, perhaps using an external hard drive?

- **Owns a flash drive.** They're lightweight, can be carried on lanyards with keys, and can transport ongoing writing assignments and projects between school and home. This means students do not need to rely on e-mailing themselves files. They will have their work with them wherever they go, whether or

TUTOR TOOLBOX

Every student should have a homework notebook or day planner. They should list daily assignments on the day they're assigned and/or due. For big projects, students should record their due dates and a series of shorter-term goals (help create these interim deadlines if they're not provided).

not they have Internet access. A flash drive can also store multi-purpose resources, such as work checklists (see pages 168–172) or a list of essential equations.

- **Has back-up plans for handing in assignments.** Unless your child has seen electronic confirmation that a file or assignment has been sent (by checking the sent message folder or receiving a confirmation e-mail from the teacher or a relevant website), your child should have a Plan B for how to turn it in. This means printing a copy and bringing it to school, e-mailing a copy of the assignment to herself, or transporting it on a flash drive.

- **Uses appropriate fonts and text sizes for typed assignments.** The default for teachers still seems to be 12-point Times New Roman font, double-spaced, but this varies from class to class. Your child should respect the school's requirements. Never encourage your child to fake a longer paper by increasing the spacing between lines, the width of the margins, or the font size (even to 12.5). These changes are obvious to teachers, and they reflect poorly on students.

- **Has tried editing on paper.** Even if your child will be turning in papers electronically, it can be beneficial to review them on paper. Be sure the computer your student uses is hooked up to a printer (if you have one) and that your child knows how to use it.

In the absence of other instructions, students should label computer files with their name, the assignment type, and the date. For example: "Ruben-Tutoring Book-August 2011.doc." Sending in a document called "My Paper" or "Big Assignment OMG" isn't a good academic move.

Organized Resistance

At the beginning of the year, you bought your child five three-subject notebooks, a three-ring binder, and a collection of multicolored paper folders. Yet all of his papers are crushed at the bottom of his backpack. Or shredded into his backpack zipper. Or half-eaten by who knows what.

Sound familiar?

If your child resists all seemingly reasonable organization efforts, consider three possibilities: (a) your child is consciously, actively rejecting organization; (b) your child is unconsciously, obliviously, or passively rejecting organization; (c) your child is emulating Buddhists, who create and immediately destroy sand mandalas to make the point that life is transitory.

In the case of (a), go for the compromise. You need your child to recognize that each step he takes toward a more orderly life will benefit him. *Giving* your child a system may not work, unless he's receptive to that plan. Collaborate.

YOU: Can we agree that your papers look like they were the victims of a wildebeest attack?

YOUR CHILD: It's not *that* bad.

YOU: Fine. Goat attack?

YOUR CHILD: Yeah.

YOU: If you were to consider upgrading from goat attack to another animal, what would it be?

YOUR CHILD: Meerkats?

YOU (*handing your child a lovely, new binder*): Fine. Would meerkats allow you to use this lovely, new binder?

YOUR CHILD: No.

YOU: What could you use instead?

YOUR CHILD (*producing a cruddy folder that will improve conditions despite looking terrible*): This cruddy folder.

YOU: Fine.

So that's it. Cruddy folder it is. Meerkats. One step at a time. If it works, upgrade to something without claws next month.

In the case of (b), find out if your child truly understands her organizational system.

If she does and intends to use it—but then doesn't follow through and isn't sure why—try to simplify the system. It's possible that there is so much going on at school that your child can't stop to think about sorting papers. As in the above case, find a temporary folder that your child can use for papers received during the school day. She can sort them at home in the evenings.

It's a red flag if your child completes homework assignments but then can't find them or forgets about them when it's time to hand them in. It's entirely possible you can resolve the disorganization with a little individualized advice, but do be aware that these are among the qualifying signs of ADD/ADHD and executive function disorders. (If you suspect or wonder if your child might have a diagnosable learning condition, speak with your child's school's guidance counselor or

---

TUTOR TOOLBOX

I've had several tutors tell me their students swear by Inspiration, software designed to help students brainstorm and organize for writing assignments: inspiration.com.

learning specialist to find out what resources or support systems they recommend.)

In the case of (c), the excuse does not count unless your child has independently provided the Buddhist ritual destruction explanation to you. And if he's done that level of research to avoid organization, he's a go-getter and will be okay in the world.

OUT WITH THE OLD

On the last day of classes, school recycling bins overflow with rejected notebooks. I've seen students dump the contents of lockers and backpacks without a second glance. Others burn notes in celebratory summer bonfires.

Granted, plenty of papers can be recycled without hesitation: completed Scantron (bubble/multiple choice) sheets that lack related questions, basic math drills for mastered skills, anything illegible. But there are a few categories of papers that your child should learn to salvage:

1. **Keepsakes and portfolio pieces.** These are projects or written work of sentimental value that exemplify a phase in your child's academic life or represent work well done, of which your child should be proud. For example, the paper where your child wrote his first full sentence. A short story he wrote in third grade about a cat from outer space. His freshman "A" research paper on the Cuban missile crisis. In a special box or file folder, save work that you or your child would enjoy seeing

---

TUTOR TOOLBOX

At the very least, a student must be able to find his papers when he needs them, whether he is searching in school or at home and whether he is looking for papers from earlier in the day or earlier in the year. If he can't do so quickly and easily, he needs to step up his organization.

again later. This is not just for the distant future; reviewing the contents of this file every year or two will remind a child that the family values his hard work and takes pleasure in his accomplishments. Also, your child will be able to see and feel good about his yearly progress.

2. **Notes of use to your child.** Your child should get in the habit of saving the most relevant notes from year to year. Many of these could be useful in later grades or in college. The same goes for annotated books.

3. **Notes of use to you or another child in your family.** As your child's tutor, you can help guide him through the process of deciding which notes, papers, and projects should get saved for use by another family member.

This winnowing of old schoolwork is a good summer project, although you might want to wait until just before school begins again, perhaps in late August. You won't have to live with the paper clutter for too long, but it will have been just enough of a break that notes can remind students of material they covered the year before and what they might need to review before the new year begins.

Where should you keep these papers? Ideally, you would separate them by grade and/or subject. File cabinets and plastic boxes are helpful tools. Another possibility is to keep one or more grades' worth of old papers standing up in an accordion file, with each pocket devoted to a different subject. You might also want to save old assignment notebooks and calendars. They serve as a journal of your child's academic career and activities, and it can be fascinating for a student to go back and see how much work he had in different grades, and what his day-to-day life involved.*

The end of the year is also a good time to take care of digital backlog. If your child has a school e-mail account, she should sort and file

---

* This will only apply to a few people, but, if you have an inkling that one of your children may grow up to be a teacher, encourage him to keep syllabi and assignment notebooks to refer to later, for lesson planning.

her messages and delete anything obsolete. If your child is lucky enough to have his own computer, he's probably going to be using the same one in the coming year, so it's important that it not be littered with virtual clutter come September.

Help your child back up the previous year's work, and store the flash drive or external hard drive in a safe location. Do this even if your child is not concerned about the possibility of his work vanishing. You're showing that you value your child's hard work and want it to last.

LET'S NOT FORGET THE MIDDLE STEP

America has taken the footpath that ARPANET blazed in 1969 and built a superhighway. Documents zip between screens with the click of a mouse. Want to buy a jogging suit, pay your credit card bill, or find directions to the zoo? No need to get to the mailbox or a map; just sit, stare, and click. Best of all, woe to those poor suckers still paying off the 1970 Britannica they ordered on layaway—today, search engines spit out information instantaneously. The Internet does it all.

But at what cost?

During a recent summer, I met with a ten-year-old girl who told me about the new American Girl doll, Rebecca Rubin, a Jewish girl from 1914. Like all American Girl dolls, Rebecca was sold with culturally relevant miniatures.

"What accessories do you think she comes with?" I asked. As an educator, I thought this was a fun chance to discuss religious culture. We could see what this student knew about the Jewish faith by brainstorming. Doll-sized dreidel? Mini-mezuzah? A little carton of Chinese food?

"Hang on." My student ran across the room to a laptop. Click. Click. Click. Before I knew it, Google had produced Rebecca Rubin's menorah. Done. We had the answer to my question in front of us.

I recalled the motto of a theater camp I attended: "It's the journey, not the product." At the time, it sounded like an excuse, in case a performance flopped. But now, when it came to Googling, I got it. While

TUTOR TOOLBOX

Look for online talks given by your child's favorite authors. Or if you know a children's book author is coming into town, have your child read the author's books so that she'll be more engaged when she hears the author speak.

the ends have their place, we can gain greater rewards by pondering the means.

My student was smart. She was also responsive. She wasn't trying to defy me by Googling. Had I asked her to think rather than click, I'm sure she would have done so happily. The point is, it wasn't her instinct.

Which, I realized, is exactly why it has to be ours. By "ours," I mean parents, teachers, and anyone else who remembers daily life before the Internet. It is our responsibility to set an example. To pause. To share and spread that long-lost middle step—the realm between wondering and knowing in which thinking, imagining, and creativity occur. This, not the click of a mouse, is the true magic.

TUTOR TAKE-AWAY

- The average child spends over seven hours a day using electronic media; thus, it pays to learn how to use new technology in constructive, educational ways.

- Recommended resources include audio books, online classes, and educational websites.

- Internet content is forever: monitor your child's online input and blog posts.

- Your GPS can be an educational tool, as can Google Maps and Google Earth.

- Be selective about movies.

- Your student's bookmarked websites should include a dictionary, a search engine, and a national news source.

- YouTube offers more than cute kittens.

- If your child turns in homework electronically, backup is essential. Consider the versatile flash drive and external hard drive.

- Don't be taken in by the myth of multitasking.

- Get your student in the organization habit—in both the physical and the digital realms.

- Salvaging some schoolwork at the end of the term will provide future rewards for both parent and child.

- Don't be overreliant on the Internet; remember the value of leisurely thought and imagination.

CHAPTER 7

How Much for an A?
The Ethical Parent-Tutor

While conducting interviews for this book, I spoke with Sara White, a Virginia mother and Shenandoah University's English as a Second Language coordinator. Sara homeschooled her two children, teaching them history while visiting battlefields and literature by reading aloud with them through their teenage years. Her life and her children's lives sounded so intertwined that I wondered how she handled the question of undue parental influence. When Sara told me about how her son started taking classes at the local community college at age fourteen, I became even more curious. After all, he was making the transition from an at-home education with an involved mother to a college environment, which traditionally expects independent work. And so I asked Sara how she knew when and where to draw the line between helping her son too much and too little. "How much help is too much help?" I wanted to know.

"If the point is helping your children learn," she said, "then you never cross the boundary."[1]

How simple: Sara's statement forms the basis for an effective litmus test for parent-tutors. When gauging your involvement in a student's academic life, ask yourself this question: "Is my primary motivation for my child to learn?"

Or has helping your child learn and become passionate about science become secondary to getting high science grades? To winning the science fair? To getting a head start on MCAT prep so that your child can become a doctor just because you're one?

If another goal has supplanted learning, be sure that the priority shift has not resulted in a willingness to overstep your bounds in helping your child. Erasing the incorrect answers on your child's math homework might allow him to write in the correct answers and get a higher grade, but is it the most effective way to help him learn to correct his own mistakes? And is it right to do?

Don't get me wrong—I think it's wonderful when students get good grades and aspire to win prizes and be doctors. But even if your child is focused on those goals and you are trying to be supportive, you as the parent-tutor must keep the bigger picture in mind. You must, above all, want your child to care about the act of learning. Weigh your decisions with that aim in mind, and everything else will come into focus.

WHOSE WORK IS IT ANYWAY?

I can think of quite a few ethical quandaries that could have been avoided by parents asking themselves a second question: "Am I completing a task in lieu of my child doing it?" Helping your child is one thing—doing work *for* your child is another. It sends the message to a child that he does not have ownership over his own educational career, which takes away motivation and pride.

And if you're changing something on an assignment when your child is not present, you're almost certainly crossing an ethical line.

If your child asks you to do something *for* her, it might be due to a lack of motivation. It could also be that your child isn't confident about her ability to grasp the task or doubts your willingness to provide sustained guidance.

You can talk your child through a difficult task by creating an example based on—but not identical to—the original. "Here's what I might do in a case like this," you can say, and then complete a similar math problem or write a sentence with a similar grammar point. Your child watches and then tries the original problem again afterward. In other words, you're modeling a skill without doing any of your child's work in her stead.

Don't Fall into the Typing Trap

I used to type papers as a motivational technique for students who felt stymied by the process of putting words on paper. During a typical writing session, I would sit at the computer, and my student would sit next to me. I would ask the student to state his ideas in complete sentences while I typed them verbatim. This approach allowed a student to produce a first draft quickly and smoothly. Later, I'd guide the student through a revision process, a writing stage that many students find more manageable than getting down an initial draft.

I felt vaguely uneasy about the process but didn't think that much of it until I saw one of these same students type a first draft himself. It was a conceptual and mechanical mess. I realized the problems with my initial approach were twofold:

1. Typing a paper for a student while prompting him to expand on particular ideas is like playing with a Ouija board. No one's ever sure who's pushing the indicator, and when it spells out a surprisingly coherent message, it's not really clear who wrote it.

2. The danger of typing for your child is that you will automatically edit your child's language. Even if you're typing your child's dictation word for word, as I tried to do, you're still

editing in that you're not making the spelling, punctuation, and grammar errors that your child might make.

Remember, if your goal is to make yourself obsolete, you need to be sure that your child can independently follow the steps needed to complete a polished writing assignment. When you're the one at the keyboard, you may find you're hindering that learning process.

If you're working with a student for whom speed is an issue, and you're already sure that the slowdown isn't caused by lack of research or preparation, have your child freewrite his drafts. Set a timer and tell your child that he can't stop writing (or typing) until the timer goes off. With this approach, students end up getting a lot of material down on paper and then can focus on cutting and revising rather than staring at a blank page.

What Is Plagiarism?

Plagiarism occurs when someone takes another person's work and passes it off as her own, either intentionally or unintentionally. It's possible to plagiarize ideas and direct language. Plagiarism can occur in a paper, in a presentation, or even on a school poster. As students come of age in the digital era, many end up plagiarizing unintentionally—they believe that freely available content on the Web can be taken without attribution.

In today's cut-and-paste world, plagiarism has become extremely easy to do. And, perhaps just as easily, it can lead to devastating results. The consequences of plagiarism and other cheating increase with age

TUTOR TOOLBOX

If you're going to type for a child, only do so as a rare motivational device. If you're typing up an assignment that your child has already written out on paper, you will be less likely to inadvertently edit what your child says.

and can be severe, ranging from suspension and failure to expulsion and the end of a college, graduate school, or professional career.

Set a good moral foundation now. If a student gets information from an outside source, it's best to acknowledge it, whether with footnotes, endnotes, or explanations in the text. Teach your child a basic principle of writing research papers: anything not in quotation marks is assumed to be her own writing, and anything without a citation is assumed to be her own original idea.

Of course, while we should be sensitive to plagiarism, there's something historically and educationally significant to the saying that "imitation is the sincerest form of flattery." More than that, imitation is necessary. As poet Mary Oliver wrote, "You would learn very little in this world if you were not allowed to imitate."[2]

Recently, I watched an online video of a friend's baby, Nate. Nate's father said, "Blub, blub, blub." Nate said, "Blub, blub, blub." Nate's father was ecstatic. We were ecstatic. Everyone was beside themselves, posting messages about how brilliant Nate was. We are thrilled when babies imitate their parents.

Some graduate schools give their creative writing students the assignment of copying the written voices of different famous writers. When we study math, we model our proofs after those of famous mathematicians. Poets learn to write Shakespearean sonnets even if they ultimately want to create new poetic forms. First we imitate, then we master and internalize the models, and then we branch out.

You can even consider encouraging imitation of your career skills. My mother had me type her editorial changes into the computer when she ghostwrote holistic health books, and I became well-versed in bioflavanoids, the benefits of juicing, and, perhaps more important, the rules of editing. One of my students recently starting talking with authority on CFCs (chlorofluorocarbons); it turned out his father was an environmentalist and had him read his briefings. The student absorbed the content and also was able to identify his father's writing style and compare it with his own. Let your children observe and participate in your activities, and you may be surprised by what they pick up.

EVALUATING INTERNET RESOURCES

When your child is conducting online research for papers, he will find the Internet to be full of wonderful sources, some reliable—and others more like shady characters in a dark alley going "Psst!"

If your child can't answer yes to all four of these questions, he might not have a usable source.

1. Did this information have to be vetted by someone other than the author (such as a newspaper fact-checker or the editor of a peer-reviewed journal)?

2. Would this source face legal or professional consequences if his or her information was inaccurate?

3. Is this a recognized, respected author or organization?

4. If you're unsure about the information provided by this source, can you find it documented somewhere else as well?

Also consider whether a source or its author is biased, meaning that the person has not mentioned, acknowledged, or considered a valid opposing view to the point being made.

The most reliable sources will be published in (print or online) encyclopedias, magazines, newspapers, scholarly journal articles, and books, as well as materials printed by established organizations. Don't rely on information found on blogs or other informal websites unless your child is specifically looking for first-person stories.

Is It True That "Wikipedia Doesn't Count?"

When my husband was in graduate school, one of his classmates once
told him to go to Wikipedia and search for "Awesome." When Adam
found the page, he learned not that awesome means "to inspire awe" but
that "Awesome is . . . [Adam's classmate's name]."

That is why "Wikipedia doesn't count" is a common teacher
refrain: because anyone can alter Wikipedia's contents and, though
results will probably be edited later for accuracy, there's no guarantee
that they'll have been edited at the moment you happen to find the
page. Wikipedia is always working to increase its accuracy, but for
now this is the reason that Wikipedia can't necessarily be used as a
legitimate source. Teaching your child to filter and judge information's
credibility is important, and Wikipedia can help teach that lesson.

Just because Wikipedia isn't usually a valid source for a paper doesn't
mean it's worthless. Rather, it's a great first source of information, as
long as you then corroborate your findings somewhere else. When I
get to a new topic, I often use Wikipedia to give myself a primer. Facts
included on Wikipedia pages have their references cited at the bottom
of the page. These links can be excellent and legitimate places to continue research.

SPARKNOTES AND CLIFFSNOTES AND GOOGLE—OH MY!

A tenth-grade student once told me, about a book, "I didn't read it, but I Googled it."

Unless a student's teacher prohibits these sources, here is when it's okay to use Google, SparkNotes, CliffsNotes, or another reference guide to provide clarification about readings:

- Only *after* an initial reading of the original source material.

- Only *after* first trying to puzzle out unclear passages by repeated readings and consultation with dictionaries, footnotes, teachers, friends, and family members. There's more to be gained from figuring out language through study and discussion than through a guidebook.

Some students review for exams by reading SparkNotes or CliffsNotes. Again, this can be useful, but only if the student has first thoroughly reviewed the book itself.

There's a satisfaction that comes from recognizing the significance of light and dark imagery in *The Scarlet Letter* or the symbolism of the carousel in *The Catcher in the Rye* on one's own, without having had a study guide reveal it first. It's also important for students to understand that there's not just one right answer when analyzing a piece of literature. Reading the "answers" in one of these little books can send the wrong message.

KEEP CHEATING IN CHECK

Here are some reasons students cheat:

- It can seem like an easy way out of studying.
- They don't realize it's wrong.
- They succumb to peer pressure.
- Their teachers don't care if they cheat.

- Desperation: they do realize cheating is wrong but are more scared of the consequences of failing—the fallout from teachers, colleges, parents, or friends—than the consequences of cheating.

Cheating could also be motivated by a combination of these factors. This seemed to be the case for a tenth-grade student who matter-of-factly informed me that, when taking tests, he completes essay portions first—he saves the multiple-choice bubbles section for last, since he "can always copy" if he runs out of time.

Here are some ways you can prevent your child from cheating:

- Don't threaten or scare your child. Your child should never be so scared of failing that he cheats. If you're sending that message, change your attitude. Teach your child that what makes you proudest are effort and moral integrity—and that cheating invalidates all that.

- Don't cheat.

- If for some reason you do—on taxes, by not telling restaurants if they've undercharged you, by using the handicapped parking spots even though you're not handicapped—don't do it in front of your child. Your "just this once" justifies your child's.

NEED HELP LANDING THAT HELICOPTER?

Okay, so you don't want to be a helicopter parent—you really, really don't. But maybe you need a little help slowing down the whirring blades and landing the darn thing. Here are four ways you can do that.

Don't Get Hung Up on Homework

It's your *child's* responsibility to know when homework is due—and, ideally, to record that information in a homework notebook. But, at least initially, you may want to provide your child with a framework for when and where to do homework.

This may mean you remind students they have homework to be done and it's time to do it. It might also mean that you discuss due dates with children in kindergarten and first grade, or, for other students, that you oversee this process all the way through the end of middle school, with an eye toward empowering your child to be self-accountable.

By high school, your child should have an independent handle on assignment due dates. For longer-term assignments, though, she may still want help plotting out shorter-term deadlines and having some accountability for meeting them.

Stop Sorting through Your Child's Backpack

Don't be a backpack detective.

For your child, having organized school papers is a sign of his respect for his school and teacher. On the other hand, for you, it's sign of respect to your child not to *snoop* through those papers. Instead, get your child involved as early as possible in organizing his own possessions. You can prompt a younger student to put homework in the appropriate folder and an older student to sort a binder's worth of papers. Model this behavior by finding a regular time to go through and organize excess paperwork in your home.

If you're a helicopter parent, try to switch aircraft. It's safer to emulate a plane in a holding pattern. You're nearby making sure conditions are clear and landing only when the ground asks you to land. Don't hover overhead like a helicopter with your rope ladder down as if you think this is a rescue mission.

TUTOR TOOLBOX

A large wall calendar can help your child keep assignment deadlines in view.

Rethink Your Involvement with Your High School Student's Teacher

I've put my child's teacher in my

❑ Speed dial

❑ Facebook friend list

❑ Car trunk

Unless you're personal friends with the teacher (or have a luxurious car trunk), if you answered yes to one or more of these, you may be an overinvolved parent. By high school—and even earlier—if your child is equipped to do so, it's preferable to have him advocate and communicate for himself.

EXCEPTIONS

- A teacher or administrator has requested direct contact with you.
- You're worried about your child and feel it's critical to speak to a professional educator.
- Your child is very uncomfortable approaching a particular teacher for some valid reason.
- Your child is not capable for some other valid reason.
- Your child is being bullied.

If you plan to talk to a middle or high school student's teacher, should you tell your child first? Yes. When a child reaches middle school—and certainly by high school—it becomes, in most cases, inappropriate to communicate with teachers without alerting your child first.

Go around a child's back and you can disempower her. Instead, you want to show your child the same level of respect you would give to another adult. If you really want to talk to a teacher about something, give your child a chance to handle the issue first and/or to let her teacher know that you'll be in touch. By doing this, you're acknowledging that your child is the architect or controller of her own education.

When I taught tenth grade, I had a policy of not speaking with any parent about particular grades or assignments unless that parent's child had approached me for a discussion first. Give yourself the same restriction and allow your high schooler to become a self-advocate.

Go Easy on the Grade Tracking

Some schools use Blackboard, Edline, or other online systems to share grading information with parents. Personally, I believe children should have sole control of that information. School is an area where children have independent jurisdiction over their lives, and they should have the right to learn to manage their own grades and know when to share that information with their parents. If your child *wants* you to monitor his grades, fine. Or if you think a child is failing and lying about it, it's a different case. Otherwise, respect your child's right to privacy. (These comments do not apply to report cards, which only come a few times a year and which parents *should* have the right to see.)

Use of these sites leads to micromanaging and unnecessary stress. When you see "4 out of 8" on a math homework assignment, you might feel compelled to question or nag about the missing four points. But it's perfectly reasonable to miss points on a homework assignment—mistakes are how we learn—and pointing it out will only make a child anxious, neurotic, and grade obsessed rather than focused on learning.

HOW MUCH FOR AN A?

In Washington, DC, in 2008, school chancellor Michelle Rhee made headlines when she announced a plan to pay middle school students for the quality and timeliness of their work, thereby challenging the old adage that learning is its own reward. Similar programs have been tested in school systems elsewhere in America, and paying for A's has, of course, been common practice in some families for generations.

In DC, the payment project led to increases in reading test scores for some students, but, beyond that, the results were inconclusive. What's more certain is the value of rewards that promote intrinsic motivation—namely, the value of verbal and intellectual rather than material rewards.

I tend to think of Rhee's system as a short-term approach for students in dire straits, as a temporary, emergency fix for a school culture in crisis. The district's results corroborated this idea, in that the students who showed the greatest improvement were those who had been suspended from school the previous year for disciplinary reasons.

Try to use nonmaterial motivators to teach your child to appreciate her daily hard work. If your child respects you, your good favor alone will be a reward. Katie McLane, the owner of Potomac Tutors, told me about the time she was tutoring a young girl who had done a good job on her work. "Oh, you did that well," Katie told her. "I think we need to celebrate." Then they got up and danced around the room.

The dancing became a regular feature within their sessions. Katie's student would ask, "Is that worth a dance?"

"You tell me," Katie would say.[3]

Soon enough, the student was able to judge her own learning and determine which triumphs merited a dance. She had developed an intuitive feel for when to reward herself.

If you're aching to issue a material reward, don't make it a reward contingent on grades. Instead, have an end-of-the-year graduation party or dinner, or another recognition of a time-based milestone.

How to Praise a Child

The right kind of praise can be a valuable reward. As recent research has shown, though, there's a particular way to praise. In *NurtureShock*, Po Bronson and Ashley Merryman lay out the new rules of praising.

First of all, don't tell your child he's "smart."[4] It turns out this is counterproductive and can be a disincentive. It teaches children of all classes, genders, and ages these lessons:

- Intelligence is inherent, and either you're smart or you're not.

- If you're smart, there's no need to do much work. If you're not, there's no hope of improvement, so why bother?

- If you've labeled a child "smart," he's going to be afraid of taking any academic risks that might lead to failure, because it could turn out he's not "smart" after all.

Instead, praise effort. Congratulate your child on his hard work. Compliment him on how dedicated he is to learning his vocabulary words. Then a low grade will not feel so dangerous, as your child sees that you appreciate the work he puts into his studying more than some alleged innate intelligence.

As Bronson and Merryman point out, if you are specific and selective in your praise, your child will know exactly what he has done so well and, by extension, what behaviors he should replicate. For example, when working with a student, I might praise his willingness to ask questions about math concepts or his desire to outline a paper before writing a draft. I might compliment his ability to explain why a teacher's particular style is hard for him to follow and tell him I'm impressed that he has come up with a plan to compensate for the confusion. If you're commenting on a behavior that is not yet habit, your words might reinforce the importance of a child's choice.

Limit your praise and provide constructive criticism. Praising unduly can give a child the sense that he has maxed out his ability. If you have a suggestion for improvement, it shows there's still room for growth. This doesn't mean you should be a perfectionist, which could drive a child crazy. Try to sense your child's own personal limits, and give a reasonable balance of comments and constructive critiques.

Here's the advice I'd give to parents on how to criticize (when reviewing a writing assignment, for example): start out with something positive, then go into the negative—using words like *confusing*, *unclear*,

---

TUTOR TOOLBOX

Rebecca Wallace-Segall, the founder of the award-winning creative writing program Writopia Lab, avoids defining her students as "good" or "bad" at composing stories. Rather, she refers to all of her students as *developing writers*.[5] Your child, too, is in the process of building skills in assorted academic areas. Remember, as long as he's putting in solid effort, he's developing in all of them.

and *awkward* rather than *bad, a mess*, and *written on the level of a sleepy kindergartner*. For example, if your child is editing a paper, you can say, "You're making such a strong point in this paragraph that you don't want your readers to get distracted by this topic sentence, which isn't about your main point. What could you do to make it more relevant?" As appropriate, follow your child's response with additional suggestions or encouraging remarks.

STICKY SITUATIONS AND HOW TO GET UNSTUCK

As mothers and fathers know, sometimes the joy of parenting seems to devolve into the challenge of problem solving. The same holds true for parent-tutors. Here's how I recommend tackling common scholastic concerns.

What to Do When a Child Fails

As long as it's not too regular, failure is a reason to celebrate (secretly). Trial and error are an important part of the educational process. Think of what you have learned from your own missteps. Your child will also learn lessons from his failure. Maybe he'll see that not studying leads to consequences. Or that the material was harder than he expected. Or that he needs to prepare differently next time.

Maybe your child's failure was even a true success. He may have had five tests and a quiz all on the same day and needed to prioritize. Perhaps he got A's and B's on all those tests except one. Is that F really so bad?

When you flub a presentation or make a social faux pas, does it help you afterward if someone berates you? No. It rarely does. You probably realize your errors shortly after making them, and I suspect you have an innate feeling that you would like to do better next time. Your child gets that same feeling the moment the teacher hands back his paper upside down so that other students can't see his D. There's no need to reinforce that sense of shame.

If your child tells you he failed a test, ask whether he expected to fail. Whatever his answer, you can ask, "Why?" or "What happened?" Then prompt your child to tell you what he might do differently in the future. Talk through a plan, and ask your child if there's any way that you can help him on his next test, paper, or assignment. If you have this discussion now, including asking your child what type of reminders he might like from you next time around, he'll be much more receptive to your gentle prompting when the time comes.

What to Ask at Back-to-School Night

Ah, back-to-school night—that rite of passage in which roomfuls of parents and teachers wear pasted-on smiles and feel like it's the first day of school all over again. How do you handle it?

Show the teacher that your family cares about the *right* kind of numbers and letters—in other words, try not to ask about grades. Instead, ask how you as a parent can support or supplement what the teacher is trying to do in the class. This shows you're involved, have your priorities straight, and want to educate your child.

When to Seek Outside Help or Tutoring

For some students, it can be useful to have an additional, outside presence to provide academic support and role modeling. When is this is a good idea?

- When there's too much baggage in the parent-child relationship, making working together academically and/or emotionally unproductive

- When academic content is far enough beyond a parent's abilities that sessions are unproductive (For more information on this situation, see "Help! I'm Clueless in Calculus," pages 176–78.)

- When a child absolutely refuses to accept assistance from his parents but clearly needs it

- When a child has a learning disorder that necessitates outside support

In general, your best bet is to find an independent tutor who is either a generalist or a specialist, depending on your child's needs. Independent tutors and those from small, boutique companies may have advantages over those at Kaplan, Score, Huntington Learning Center, or Sylvan. If you go with a big company, find out about the tutor-to-student ratio, whether the company is willing to use materials provided by your child's school (as opposed to their own curricula), and whether you are required to sign a contract that commits your child to a certain number of sessions. Also ask your child's teachers, school learning specialists, and other parents for tutor recommendations.

Having Respect for Outside Tutors

I was working with a junior who was revising a recent paper when she said, "My mother asked if you could provide some quotes to support the paper." I was taken aback on two counts:

1. Students should never ask tutors or teachers to do work for them.

2. Parents should never ask children to ask outside tutors or teachers to do work for them.

In other words, you, as your child's tutor, should not do your child's work for her or ask anyone else to do it.

I told my student, "If you come up with possible quotes, I'd be happy to tell you which I think are the best. I don't think it would be right for me to search for quotes for you, though." The student understood, and she didn't ask me to complete work for her again.

When Something's Gotta Give

Is it okay to . . .

    . . . skip a homework assignment . . .

    . . . turn in a paper late . . .

    . . . miss school . . .

For . . .

> . . . a favorite TV show?
>
> . . . a sibling's guitar recital?
>
> . . . extra sleep?
>
> . . . play practice?
>
> . . . a funeral?
>
> . . . a vacation?
>
> . . . seeing a friend from out of town?
>
> . . . college visits?
>
> . . . the State of the Union address?
>
> . . . Take Our Daughters and Sons to Work Day?

Part of a student's education occurs when he learns how to recognize when a social, emotional, or physical need is more important than an academic obligation, and part of your role as a parent-tutor is to pay attention to the trade-offs that your child is making. Eventually, our lives get complicated, and something has to slide. Your child is facing his own equivalent of the opportunity costs you confront daily when choosing between staying late at work, vacuuming your home, and singing your child a bedtime song. Guide your child as he weighs his priorities and decides which school-related sacrifices are acceptable.

TUTOR TOOLBOX

But those who've had failures are valued, too—sometimes even more so. Start-up companies often prefer to hire a chief executive with a failed start-up in his or her background. The person who failed often knows how to avoid future failures. The person who knows only success can be more oblivious to all the pitfalls.

—Randy Pausch, *The Last Lecture*

When considering trade-offs, a child should think about what motivates his interest in each of his options. What will the short-term and long-term consequences of each choice be? Is this a recurring issue (e.g., signing up for a time-consuming extracurricular activity), in which case the consequences are persistent, or a one-time event (e.g., attending a protest) and less likely to yield larger academic problems? On which side of the decision will regret lie?

Badmouthing

- Don't badmouth your child's teacher.
- Don't badmouth other students.
- Don't badmouth yourself.

I spoke with one mother who said she used to hear homeschooling parents talking negatively about their own abilities to other parents, with their kids in earshot. "I have no idea what I'm doing. We're just getting by," they would say. Making this kind of statement erodes the confidence that your child has in you. Whether homeschooling or tutoring, avoid putting down your own abilities (at least in earshot of your child).

Likewise, do not put down your own child. I've had other tutors tell me about parents who introduce their child with, "This is the laziest child. Besides that, she's a good kid." A good tutor would never introduce or identify a child with a permanent-sounding, negative label. If you want to identify what your child needs to work on, that's fine. But avoid giving that deficit a pejorative label.

Put forth confidence in yourself and your child. And show respect to everyone else.

What If a Child Is Not Capable of Getting Good Grades?

Either that's true—in which case you can refocus on learning instead of grade-based academics and help guide your child toward a lifelong passion, thinking about what she might eventually want to do as a career—or

Let's not make a deal: try to avoid negotiating with your child. If you change your mind about something due to your child's entreaties or arguments, make it clear that you are changing because of your child's *reasoning*, not because you're compromising your principles or giving in due to frustration.

it's not true. Maybe your child isn't getting "good" grades due to your doubts or her own doubts. Maybe your child is struggling to get "good" grades at this particular school or with this course load and would benefit from a switch—*or* would benefit more from staying and getting slightly lower grades than you would like.

Here's the question: is your child dissatisfied with her grades? If she would be perfectly fine with the B or C that she's working hard to get, back off.

What If a Child Wants to Read Below-Grade-Level Materials?

One afternoon, I was browsing in the children's section at Politics & Prose, an independent bookstore in Washington, DC. Nearby, a mother and her two young children looked for books. The boy selected one, and his choice clearly made his mother unhappy. "That's below your level," she said. "I'm not getting that for you." The boy and his mother argued, his behavior deteriorated, and she eventually dragged him away in a huff.

Though I don't know all the particulars of this mother-child relationship, I suspect this mother was making a common assumption: her son would not learn from books that were "below" his reading or grade level. Telling a child not to read a book he loves that's too "easy" is degrading and will destroy a child's passion. Are you also saying that illustrations can be outgrown? What if your child is going to be an artist and likes looking at pictures? Or a literary agent and is absorbing the qualities of children's books?

Imagine if we only ever played music that was slightly too hard or ate food that was slightly too spicy or lifted weights that were slightly too heavy. Granted, we might be better piano players, our taste buds might evolve, and we'd have bigger muscles. But would we ever feel mastery over any of these areas?

Your child is probably not consciously trying to build expertise. Rather, he might be reading for pleasure, because he likes the story, because he finds it comforting, or because it makes him feel good to know it so well. But in the process, he is building skills.

Here's what you can do. If your child is reading books that you think are too easy for him (or even if he's not), find all the other books you can by the same author, and have your child read all of them, if he's enjoying them. Say your ten-year-old keeps rejecting the summer reading books you have brought him and just wants to flip through his little sister's copy of Eric Carle's book *The Very Hungry Caterpillar*. Find *Do You Want to Be My Friend?* and *Pancakes, Pancakes!* and *The Grouchy Ladybug* and all the other Eric Carle books you can. Have your child read them all. Or your seventeen-year-old only wants to read Kate DiCamillo's *The Tale of Despereaux*. Have the teen read all of DiCamillo's books, no matter how simple they seem to you. Then do the following:

- Engage your children in conversations about Carle and DiCamillo's books. Having seen all their work, what do these authors do well? You can read the books as well to have a better sense of what appeals to your children about them and be able to have a more informed discussion.

- Challenge your children to write stories in the same style as Carle and DiCamillo.

- Learn about the authors themselves. Find articles by and about Carle and DiCamillo and give them to your children to read. You may also be able to find video clips of them talking about the books your child has read.

- Have your children compose letters to the authors, expressing reactions to the books.

By the end of the summer, you might have a ten-year-old who's only read Eric Carle, but he'll be a ten-year-old who can say, "I like the way Eric Carle uses bright shapes, animal characters, and collage illustrations." Nor should you say a book is too hard. There's nothing wrong with a challenge. A child reading a book completely out of his depth will put the book down on his own anyway.

PROFESSIONAL TUTORS' ETHICS RULES

The National Tutoring Association provides its professional tutors with a code of ethics, which includes the following pledges:

- "I understand that my role as a tutor is to never do the student's work for him or her."

- "I will give honest feedback to the student I serve and will not insult my student with false hope or empty flattery; I will always demonstrate faith in my student's learning abilities."

- "I recognize that I may not have all the answers to student questions. In this event, I will seek assistance in finding answers to the student's questions and/or direct the student to an appropriate resource for the information."

- "I understand that my ultimate goal is to assist my student in learning how he or she best learns and to help my student develop the skills to achieve his or her best, most efficient learning."

- "I expect to learn along with my student."[6]

Do you already follow these guidelines when you interact with your child? Are there ways you could apply them more effectively?

TUTOR TAKE-AWAY

- Good grades are great, but fostering learning should be your big-picture goal.

- Do not complete your child's tasks for him; rather, model the skills that he will need to do so himself.

- Let your student type her own papers.

- Plagiarism is the use of another's work without attribution, and it is wrong.

- When doing research, your child should evaluate the reliability of Internet sources.

- Wikipedia is a good jumping-off point, as opposed to a valid resource.

- Students should read the original literature before consulting study guides.

- Empower your child to be self-accountable regarding homework.

- Respect your child's privacy vis-à-vis the contents of his backpack as well as his day-to-day grades.

- It is better to praise a student's effort than to praise her innate qualities.

- There is an upside to failure.

- - - - - - - - - - -

CHAPTER 8

Points of Contact:
Parent-Tutored Teens

When the mother of a high school student called the tutoring company where I worked to set up an appointment before her son's precalculus test, I asked her if she knew what the test was on. "Are you crazy, honey?" the mother said. "I can't even read the first page."

Later, a different mother called to set up science tutoring for her high school daughter. When I asked what science class her daughter was in, she said, "What do you mean?" I explained to this woman that, based on the school's offerings, her daughter was in a biology, chemistry, or physics class. "I'll have to check," she said.

I knew that both of these mothers cared about their children and were dedicated to their well-being, so their lack of knowledge about their children's academics bothered me. Here's the thing: as your child transitions from primary school to middle and high school, he changes—and as a result, you may find it hard to stay as involved in the particulars of his life. After all, you no longer need to monitor play dates, sign permission slips, or walk your child to the schoolhouse door. Your child's autonomy and personal academic accountability increase (or should, at least) as the amount of interaction you have with his teachers decreases.

But it's crucial that you still find a way to stay engaged in your child's life and to provide guidance. If your spouse works in a field you don't understand, you still make an effort (I hope) to ask what type of project he or she is working on now. Likewise, you should know what subjects your child is studying and ask what's new in different classes.

If you're the parent-tutor—or even just the parent—of a teenager, I would guess that you spend much of your time thinking about two goals:

1. Helping your child succeed in high school

2. Helping your child succeed after high school

I would argue that a third, often overlooked goal should perhaps come first.

3. Finding common ground

Professional tutors develop relationships with their students. As part of that effort, they strive to find a nonacademic common ground with each student. As your child grows and changes, it can happen that your child's interests are now outside your or your partner's realm of knowledge and that your communication falters.

This breakdown may affect a student's emotional, social, and academic well-being. More important, consider that when your child leaves home, you want to have maximized the positive personal connections in your relationship, to give your child a solid emotional base.

So, before you get to the schoolwork, identify at least one communication-friendly activity that you share with your child. (Your spouse or partner should do likewise.)

What does "communication-friendly" mean? It means that before, during, or after the activity, you and your child will spend time interacting with just one another, one on one—an interaction that could (*could*, which does not mean it always *does*) lead to a prolonged discussion.

You could share:

- **A physical activity:** walking, running, biking, swimming, boating, skating, rock climbing, bowling, taking the dog to the park

- **A hobby or art:** gardening, cooking, baking, knitting, crocheting, beading, painting, embroidering, scrapbooking

- **An event in the community:** volunteering to collect litter, exploring restaurants, taking trips to museums, zoos, or historical sites

Whether you spend time with your child outside of your home or in it, it's important that he not feel rushed. This is helpful both in your shared activity *and* in the tutoring relationship. Your child should not get the sense that you want to be somewhere else or that your attention is divided.

Journalists and interviewers are told to leave a little bit of extra silence when asking a question, as it allows the subject to think and then to answer more fully. You can employ this same technique. While asking questions might not be intuitive for you and may even require preplanning, the act is important because it signals your interest in your child's life.

When you are out of questions, show your continued interest with your presence. Engaging in a preestablished activity gives you a reason to spend silent time together and not to end a potential conversation before it's had the chance to begin. Your child may not think he has anything to say until faced with fifteen minutes of otherwise silent time.

The foundation of a good tutoring relationship is trust. Even if tutoring in a traditional sense does not work out, spending time together helps you build a strong connection with your child. And, in the process, you've created an environment in which you and your child can share thoughts and knowledge.

KEEP READING ALOUD

Many young children have parents who read to them, but it's rare to find a middle school or high school student's family that shares reading as they did in elementary school.

In March 2010, the *New York Times* printed a story about a father and daughter who had maintained what they referred to as "The Streak," a 3,218-night, nine-year stretch during which the father read aloud to the daughter nightly. This reading streak lasted from when the daughter was in fourth grade until she left for college. In addition to providing positive memories, their tradition yielded a collection of seven hundred high-quality books, a Rowan University English major with a 3.94 GPA, and a "shared language" filled with references from Seuss to Shakespeare.

I spoke with a mother who confirmed that she had seen shared language emerge in her own family. Reading aloud provided her family with references, analogies, catchphrases, inside jokes, and other "points of contact." As an example, she used *The Pearl*, a novel by John Steinbeck. Because the family had read the book aloud, they could describe someone's actions as similar to the way that "Kino threw his pearl into the sea." They all understood that they were talking about a person who had to make the decision to give up a belonging that seemed to be of great value in order to salvage another aspect of his life. By reading together, the family had developed a verbal shorthand that augmented their relationships *and* allowed the children to practice making the type of references and connections that facilitate advanced literary and historical analysis.

As Jim Trelease says in his classic, *The Read-Aloud Handbook*, "Almost as big a mistake as not reading to children at all is stopping too soon."[1] If parents want to convince their older children that reading is pleasurable, it helps to create and share a positive experience that sends that message. For ideas on books to read aloud, see *What to Read When: The Books and Stories to Read with Your Child—and All the Best Times to Read Them* (Avery Trade, 2009) by Pam Allyn, and the tome *1001 Children's Books You Must Read Before You Grow Up* (Universe, 2009) by Julia Eccleshare. You can also consult your local librarians and booksellers,

TUTOR TOOLBOX

Nikki Bravo, the mother of a ninth-grader, recommends organizing book swaps as a way to keep students reading for pleasure at an age when many students give up the habit. Bravo invited her son's friends to bring their favorite books to her house. The boys described their books to each other and then traded.

who are generally repositories of valuable advice on classics and recently published works alike.

By the way, poetry and plays are forms of literature that just beg to be read aloud; your family members might enjoy taking turns reading their favorite poems to each other.

NOTES ON NOTE TAKING

While younger students in classroom settings are provided more explicitly with notes—often copying directly from the board—older students may be expected to take notes from class discussions and lectures. For many students, this is a completely new skill.

Students who fall behind in their reading will be at a disadvantage here, which makes advance preparation all the more crucial. If you can focus your tutoring sessions on reading material *before* it is covered in class, your child will have less to write down during lectures—and, more important, because she is already familiar with the material, she'll be able to retain more and make more connections as the teacher speaks.

You'll also need to show your child how best to take in-class notes. Emphasize that it's only necessary to write down material that was not covered in the readings. Teach your child to focus on anything the teacher emphasizes.

Students should also provide context for notes they're copying from the board that might not be clear upon rereading—otherwise you'll end up hearing, "I wrote this down, but I don't know what it means." Notes should be written in such a way that their significance will be clear days, or even months, later.

And don't let your child fall into the trap of trying to write *everything* down. The teacher may deliver a lecture at 150 words per minute, but it's not likely that your child can write more than twenty to thirty words per minute. Make sure your child knows to listen and select only the important points to record.

Though your child may already surpass you in this arena by virtue of his experience writing text messages, you can also work on a system of abbreviations to facilitate fast note-taking. Help your child identify the words that she uses most frequently when taking notes. Why write out "*Great Expectations*" when it's faster to use "*GE*"? If this week's history focus is Charlemagne, your child can save time by just writing "Charlemagne" once and writing "C" every time thereafter. Shorten words ("from" becomes "fr.") and skip vowels ("skp vwls"). Symbols also save time: if one historical event led to another, show that relationship with an arrow instead of words. Students can create a key or glossary to keep track of abbreviations that might not be self-explanatory.

How to Mark a Book

"The marked book is usually the thought-through book," writes Mortimer J. Adler, the author of *How to Read a Book*, in his 1941 essay "How to Mark a Book."[2] As students encounter more complicated reading, whether book-length or shorter, they can benefit from active reading.

Adler advocates the following techniques:

- Underline (or highlight) major points.

- Add a vertical line in the margin to doubly emphasize a previously underlined section.

TUTOR TOOLBOX

Speed reading should not be a student's goal. Rather, he should strive for engagement and comprehension.

As Adler points out, students can annotate using smaller pieces of paper (e.g., sticky notes) that fit inside the book so that they don't have to write on the pages. (This technique will be useful if your child does not own the book he's reading.)

As a parent-tutor, you can tell at a glance whether your child is annotating his reading. If not, make sure he knows how (and why) it's helpful).

- Write a "star, asterisk, or other doo-dad" in the margin to draw attention to the reading's most essential points. He also suggests dogearing the marked pages. (I prefer to write their numbers on the inside of the book's front cover.)

- Circle key words or phrases. (I also recommend that students use circles, boxes, or question marks for words they want to look up later.)

- Write in the margin any questions that occur to you while reading or simplifications of complicated points in the text.

CHECK UP ON CHECKLISTS

If your child revises a paper by scrolling up and down through computer pages, flipping through papers haphazardly, or looking generally befuddled, she may benefit from a writing checklist.

In *The Checklist Manifesto* (Picador, 2011), author Atul Gawande describes the benefits of using checklists before surgery to ensure that medical teams do not overlook easily forgettable but crucial checks. Even though some surgeons balked at the implication that they needed something so basic, there proved to be a significant reduction in errors when they used checklists. Likewise, students can use checklists to enhance their performance and ensure that they haven't missed anything.

Below is the template for my expository writing checklist, which is the checklist I use most often with students. This is a fairly comprehensive list. I recommend having a student create a condensed, personalized list that includes the elements that she tends to forget. This list can and should be adapted to make it appropriate for different classes, subjects, and ages.

After the expository paper checklist, I have included shorter lists applicable to personal essays and fiction and to math homework.

Sample Checklist: Expository Paper

OPENING

❏ Is your first sentence compelling?

❏ Is your background information relevant?

❏ Have you provided context when referencing works or characters? (For example, have you provided the title, author, and genre of a literary work or an identifying word or two about any named characters or historical figures?)

THESIS STATEMENT

❏ Does your thesis statement make an argument?

❏ Is it analytical (as opposed to a summary or an unsubstantiated opinion), telling *how* or *why* something is true?

❏ Could someone come up with a plausible counterargument? (You want the answer to be yes, as it means you're arguing a case and not just making an obvious statement.)

❏ Does your thesis statement hint at the structure of the paper?

TOPIC SENTENCES

❏ Are your topic sentences analytical?

❏ Do they tie back to your thesis statement?

❏ Do they lead smoothly into their paragraphs?

❏ When read in order, do the topic sentences give the sense of logical progression, as if the writer is a lawyer arguing a case?

❏ Do you acknowledge the counterargument somewhere in the body paragraphs?

❏ Is everything in a given body paragraph relevant to the topic sentence?

EVIDENCE (EXAMPLES AND QUOTES)

For each piece of evidence, did you:

❏ *Introduce* the evidence with appropriate context?

❏ *Insert* the evidence appropriately? (Quotes should be connected to surrounding prose and not just dropped in.)

❏ *Interpret* and explain the significance of the evidence?

❏ Are all quotes cited?

CONCLUSION

❏ Have you reiterated your thesis?

❏ Have you summarized your key points?

❏ Did your ending leave the reader with a question or deeper thought to consider?

THROUGHOUT THE PAPER

❏ Have you included the title and author of any book or other work mentioned?

❏ The first time a name is mentioned, do you provide a few words of explanation or description about that character or historical figure?

❏ Are you using the third-person point of view consistently ("he," "she" or "it" rather than "I" or "you")?

❏ Are you writing in the present tense (for English analysis) or past tense (for history analysis)?

❏ Have you avoided unnecessary repetition?

❏ Have you written concisely?

❏ Are your verbs active and varied?

❏ Is your sentence structure varied?

❏ Is your language formal and scholarly enough?

- ❏ Is your language precise enough?
- ❏ Have you written out all your contractions ("don't" as "do not," etc.)?
- ❏ Have you avoided "qualifying" phrases ("sort of," "somewhat," "a bit," etc.)?
- ❏ Have you read the paper aloud to catch mistakes?

Sample Checklist: Personal Essay or Fiction

- ❏ Is the world the characters inhabit believable and internally consistent?*
- ❏ Is something at stake?
- ❏ Is there dramatic tension?
- ❏ Do we, as readers, care about the characters?
- ❏ Is the point of view consistent?
- ❏ Is the use of tense consistent?
- ❏ Does the story use figurative language creatively?
- ❏ Does the story achieve emotional, intellectual, and artistic depth?**

---

* I once taught a student who wrote a fiction story that took place in the real world—but when a character wanted, say, money or a baby outfit, the objects simply floated by for the characters to grab. Kids do this often, and while such fantasy has creative value, the real challenge with creativity is defining a fantasy world in which the rules are clear and adhered to.

** These were criteria of good writing emphasized by Mary Collins, my graduate school advisor at the Johns Hopkins University, though she had applied them to nonfiction writing.

Sample Checklist: Math Homework

❏ Have I shown all my work?

❏ Have I checked my answers?

❏ Did I do the correct problems?

❏ Did I do *all* the problems?

❏ Do I understand and remember all the equations?

❏ Do I understand the concepts behind the problems I solved?

COMMUNICATING WITH RESPECT

When I taught tenth grade, students sent me e-mails with no greetings, closings, or thanks, and with incorrect spelling and grammar. Granted, I'm a laid-back, please-call-me-by-my-first-name kind of instructor, but I do think there's a certain etiquette that students should follow when initiating written communication with teachers, administrators, college representatives, job interviewers, and other adults. Having vetted correspondence written by tutoring position applicants and talked with people responsible for hiring elsewhere, I can say that a surprisingly small number of people can write a message that will make a good enough first impression to get their job applications taken seriously.

Don't let your child unwittingly make a bad impression in written communication. In ten minutes, you can teach him how to correspond politely.

TUTOR TOOLBOX

Writopia Lab's founder, Rebecca Wallace-Segall, encourages parents to get excited whenever their children are "narrating," whether they're writing fiction, telling the story of their day at school, or describing the plot of a movie or video game. All these forms of storytelling ultimately lead students to a better understanding of how to craft a compelling piece of writing.

Here are the essential components of an e-mail:

- **Greeting word:** Dear, Hi, or Hello
- **Title (if needed) + name:** Mr./Ms./Mrs./Miss + name (spelled correctly). Once your child has developed an e-mail rapport with a teacher, she might find it's appropriate to write messages without a greeting word or name. In deciding this, your child should follow her teacher's lead. When someone has seniority in age or position (as a teacher generally does), his or her level of e-mail formality should be met by the student. Also, your child should pay attention to the way her teacher signs an e-mail, in case it's different from the way she's been addressing the teacher.
- **Punctuation mark:** There should be a comma (less formal) or colon (more formal) after the message recipient's name.
- **Message:** Here's where your child writes the message. It should be short and specific; use proper punctuation, capitalization, spelling (no text talk), and grammar; and be broken into paragraphs to indicate separate points.
- **Thanks:** This is where your child acknowledges and appreciates that someone is helping her: "Thank you for your time," "I appreciate your time," "Thank you," "Thanks."
- **Closing:** "Best," "Thanks," "Thank you," or "Sincerely"
- **Name:** Your child should sign her e-mails the way she wants to be addressed in class. If your child's name is not in her e-mail address (e.g., crypticstudent2931@e-mail.com), it's particularly important that she identify herself. Even if it *is* in her e-mail address, it's polite to include a name.

If your child is writing an old-fashioned pencil-to-paper note, she should follow the same basic format but remember to include a date and, if needed, the time that the message was written. E-mails and voicemails record this automatically, but notes obviously do not.

As a general rule, students should not contact teachers to ask for information that they could find elsewhere.

Phone Tag

Here are some guidelines for when your child calls a teacher (or, really, anyone):

- **Greeting:** "Hi, this is [*name*]."
- **Request:** "May I please speak with [*name*]?" or "I'm calling for [*name*]."
- **Identification:** "I'm one of his students."
- **Thanks:** "Thanks."
- **Leaving information:** In the case that the intended recipient of the call is not home, a student should remember to leave both his name and phone number if he'd like a call back. If he is leaving a message on an answering machine or voicemail message (particularly if he is calling from a cell phone), he should repeat his name and phone number slowly and clearly: "Again, this is [*name*], and my home phone number is . . . ." Even if your child is leaving a message on a cell phone, he should leave his number and not say, "Call me back at this number." The person who receives the message may be getting a slew of messages and lose track of which number called. When leaving a message on an answering machine (as opposed to a cell phone), it's also polite to tell the time of the call.

Talking the Talk

Teach your student the basics of talking politely to adults. Mastering two easy steps will allow your child to create a powerful positive impression on teachers, principals, interviewers, and other parents.

1. RESPOND.

ADULT: How are you?

STUDENT: I'm doing well.

Better yet, respond politely.

ADULT: How are you?

STUDENT: I'm doing well, thanks.

For the full effect, accompany your response with eye contact and a pleasant expression. Try to show enjoyment about speaking with the other person.

2. RECIPROCATE.

Once a student has provided a response, the most socially aware among them reciprocate. It looks like this:

ADULT: How are you?

STUDENT: I'm doing well, thanks. How are you?

Reciprocating is even more impressive when it requires remembering and then rephrasing a question from earlier in the conversation.

ADULT: What did you do over spring break?

(*Conversation about hiking ensues.*)

STUDENT: And did you enjoy your break?

A student who reciprocates shows that he cares about your conversation—or at least that he cares about appearing to care, which can be just as effective.

TUTOR TOOLBOX

If you'd like to read more on academic manners, you might be interested in Ron Clark's book *The Essential 55: An Award-Winning Educator's Rules for Discovering the Successful Student in Every Child* and its companion workbook. It's a little heavy on the *ma'ams* and *sirs* for my liking, but it includes a slew of other worthwhile and thoughtful tips, such as "Rule 27: Do not stare at a student who is being reprimanded."[3]

HELP! I'M CLUELESS IN CALCULUS

What can you do when your child's knowledge has surpassed yours?

First, congratulate yourself. Your child is better off than you are. You're living the American dream!

Next, determine whether you can become versed enough in your child's work to continue your academic tutoring. A quick review of your child's class notes and textbook(s) may suffice. This preparation will often be all that's needed for you to know enough to ensure that your child's studies are on track. If your child has advanced questions about a subject, though, you'll likely need to study the material more closely.

If you find yourself completely incapable of understanding what your child is studying—for example, if you speak Italian but your child needs help with upper-level Chinese—finding outside help may be a legitimate move. Supplemental help can also be a viable option if you do have the capability of learning the material but don't have the time. This support doesn't necessarily have to come from a professional tutor you pay. From student study groups to online resources, a wide range of academic support systems exist that you and your child can put in place for higher-level support. Some possible resources follow.

Methods That Your Child Facilitates

- **Staying after school to see the teacher.** This is the default means of clarifying any content that a student can't figure out after attending class and reviewing at home. It's also the principal way a student should get information about due dates, assignment requirements, and preparation for texts and quizzes, unless the teacher has specified that students find that information online.

- **Studying with friends.** This method is generally easy to coordinate and potentially a great motivator. The students who understand a topic can explain it to the students who are struggling, a process that increases understanding for everyone. Be careful, though, because in some settings, studying with friends will prompt students to rush and miss concepts and to copy answers from friends who work more quickly.

- **Books or study guides.** These resources are available at the library, bookstore, and online. They can be an excellent way for a student to get an additional perspective on a subject.

- **Online courses and resources.** Among the almost limitless resources available on the Web, students can find academic support options that range from paying for full classes or individual lessons (such as at YourTeacher.com, for math) to using free YouTube videos to reinforce concepts.

- **Peer-to-peer tutoring.** Some schools or towns offer student-run tutoring services. If your child prefers being tutored by a classmate rather than by an authority figure, this option can work well. Plus, peer tutors have the advantage of recently having taken (and, generally, recently having succeeded in) your child's classes, so the material is fresh in their minds.

Methods That You Facilitate

- **Professional tutors.** You can find independent or company-based tutors. Select a generalist or specialist, depending on your child's needs. (See "When to Seek Outside Help or Tutoring," pages 154–55, for more information.)

- **Hiring a teacher from another school to help your child.** This option allows your child to combine the benefits of teaching expertise with the intimacy of tutoring. Schools generally have policies against students being formally tutored by their own teachers, but your child's teacher may be able to recommend another teacher (from the same or another school, depending on policy) to help your child. Or you can independently contact a particular academic department (at your child's or another school) to look for a teacher-tutor.

- **Hiring a college or graduate school student proficient in the subject.** College students tend to be cheaper than professional tutors, and they're not committed to as many (if any) students, which means they may be able to focus more on personalizing their preparation for your child. If you're at a loss for how to advertise for this type of tutor, try contacting a relevant academic department at a university or the school's graduate student organization. Of course, being a subject specialist does not always mean a college student is a good tutor, so try to find someone with tutoring or teaching experience. If your local college has an education department, you can try to find a student there who can serve as a tutor.

- **Asking (or having your child ask) your child's school what resources they recommend.** Your child's teachers, guidance counselor, or advisor might have thoughts on what supplemental materials or support systems would best assist your child.

Again, if you find outside support for your child, you have not shirked your responsibility as a parent-tutor—you have fulfilled it. Your goal all along is to engage with your child intellectually while providing him with the academic support and motivation he needs to feel excited and successful about learning. Varied paths and levels of involvement will lead you to that same outcome.

As a parent-tutor, what you're doing is simple: you're showing *you* love learning, that you love when anyone *near you* learns, and, most of all, that you love when your *child* learns. You're finding ways to help your child become a better independent learner, both by helping him determine what does work for him and by pinpointing what does not. You should—and *can*—be a crucial figure in your child's academic life. And you'll both be better for it.

TUTOR TAKE-AWAY

- Stay involved with your teen and his schoolwork, even if you don't formally tutor.

- Reading aloud still has advantages.

- Help your high-schooler hone his note-taking skills.

- Annotating books facilitates understanding.

- Checklists can aid students in polishing both writing and math assignments.

- Practicing good communication skills—over the Internet, over the phone, and in person—will provide a big boost to your teen's future success.

Resources

Y ou're bound to find materials to suit your child's particular needs as you explore bookstores and libraries, talk to other parents, and browse the Internet. The following is a list of resources that you might be less likely to encounter on your own and that could prove useful.

EDUCATION: TEACHING

The Essential 55: An Award-Winning Educator's Rules for Discovering the Successful Student in Every Child, by Ron Clark (Hyperion, 2004). A primer on academic manners by the 2001 Disney Teacher of the Year. Rules remind students to make eye contact, not to brag about scholarly successes, and not to stare at students being reprimanded.

There Are No Shortcuts, by Rafe Esquith (Anchor, 2004). An account of how Esquith, a National Medal of the Arts recipient, has motivated his fifth-grade class to work long days and perform a complete Shakespeare production each year (as featured in the documentary *The Hobart Shakespeareans*).

Teach Like Your Hair's on Fire: The Methods and Madness Inside Room 56, by Rafe Esquith (Penguin, 2007). In Esquith's second book, intended for parents and teachers, he provides insight into the particular educational techniques and exercises that he recommends.

Cheaper by the Dozen, by Frank B. Gilbreth, Jr., and Ernestine Gilbreth Carey (HarperCollins, 2005). Now a classic, this humorous 1948 memoir describes life for twelve children raised by professional efficiency experts, both of whom held a strong appreciation for the role parents can play in academic motivation.

EDUCATION: HOMESCHOOLING AND UNSCHOOLING RESOURCES (APPROPRIATE FOR ANY PARENT)

The Well-Trained Mind: A Guide to Classical Education at Home, by Susan Wise Bauer and Jessie Wise (W.W. Norton, 2009). This book is a staple for any parent. It provides advice on education from birth through the end of high school, both for homeschoolers *and* for parents who want to supplement their children's schooling with "after-schooling." *The Well-Trained Mind* has an online forum with extensive education information. (welltrainedmind.com/forums)

I would also recommend the materials published by Wise Bauer's publishing company, Peace Hill Press, which sells individual books and packages for parents who intend to homeschool and also has a Facebook page.

The Story of the World: History for the Classical Child, by Susan Wise Bauer (Peace Hill Press, 2007). Peace Hill Press offers this series of world history books, which are written in accessible narrative and could easily be used to supplement traditional schooling or for bedtime or in-car readings.

The Well-Educated Mind: A Guide to the Classical Education You Never Had, by Susan Wise Bauer (W.W. Norton, 2003). After an eloquent explanation of how to read and analyze, Bauer provides lists of recommended classics organized in chronological order by genre. Useful for motivated older students or a parent-student duo that would like to read and discuss the same books.

Dumbing Us Down: The Hidden Curriculum of Compulsory Schooling, by John Taylor Gatto (New Society, 2002). After being named New York State Teacher of the Year in 1991, Gatto went on to denounce America's education system and promote the practice of unschooling.

Teach Your Own: The John Holt Book of Homeschooling, by John Holt (Da Capo, 2003). A staple of the homeschooling movement by one of its chief proponents.

Home Education Magazine (homeedmag.com). *HEM* offers homeschooling advice to parents. Get a sense of the publication through its online archives. You can also join the magazine's Facebook group, which provides links to recommended articles and educational resources.

KONOS (konos.com). This popular homeschooling curriculum is hands-on and designed for all ages. (Its signature activity is the creation of a human-ear model under the dining table.) The materials are "biblically based," though creator Jessica Hulcy says they can be easily adapted. KONOS is used by homeschooling parents and by grandparents looking for educational activities to use with their grandchildren.

The Old Schoolhouse Magazine (thehomeschoolmagazine.com). This magazine offers advice to home educators. Please be aware that *TOS* is an openly Christian publication with language that may be off-putting, depending on your beliefs. If you follow the magazine's Facebook page, you'll be able to find information and advice that would be applicable to any educator.

The One-Year Adventure Novel (oneyearnovel.com). Designed as an English curriculum for eighth- through twelfth-grade homeschoolers, this could also be a fantastic supplemental program for any teenage student (or even a college student). It could also be used by a group of students who gather as an informal afterschool club at someone's house and each complete a writing project. A series of DVD lessons, readings, and exercises teach students about the structure of adventure novels; students outline their novels by the end of the first semester and complete a novel draft by the end of the second semester. The company will provide a sample DVD lesson for free.

Vocabulary from Classical Roots, by Lee Mountain, Norma Fifer, and Nancy Flowers (Educators Pub Service, 1998). This workbook series teaches vocabulary through word roots and can be used for students (and adults) of any age, including those trying to build word skills for standardized tests.

Rainbow Resource Center (rainbowresource.com). An in-print and online catalogue for homeschooling books and supplies.

"Ken Robinson says schools kill creativity" (ted.com/talks/ken_robinson_says_schools_kill_creativity.html). Creativity expert Sir Ken Robinson speaks about the value of creativity and the arts, the diversity of intelligence, and the reasons we need to rethink education worldwide.

The Complete Home Learning Source Book: The Essential Resource Guide for Homeschoolers, Parents, and Educators Covering Every Subject from Arithmetic to Zoology, by Rebecca Rupp (Three Rivers, 1998). Organized by subject, this extensive reference guide provides ideas and resources appropriate for students schooled in or out of the home.

Home Learning Year by Year: How to Design a Homeschool Curriculum from Preschool Through High School, by Rebecca Rupp (Three Rivers, 2000). Grade by grade, Rupp lists skills that students should have and the age-relevant books, magazines, science kits, and other educational resources that homeschoolers might want to use. Though intended for homeschoolers, this book could serve any parent well.

The Unschooling Unmanual, by Jan Hunt et al. (Natural Child Project, 2008). A collection of essays by eight authors discussing their thoughts on unschooling.

PARENTING

Sparks: How Parents Can Help Ignite the Hidden Strengths of Teenagers, by Peter L. Benson, PhD (Jossey-Bass, 2008). I like the concept of this book, which is that parents should help their children identify what is special about them—their passion, or spark. What really caught my eye is the list in the back of this book of areas where your child's passion might rest (e.g., poetry, student government, making people laugh). As of 2010, the list was also available online (ignitesparks.com/sparks_list.html).

The Big Book of Parenting Solutions: 101 Answers to Your Everyday Challenges and Wildest Worries, by Michele Borba, EdD (Jossey-Bass,

2008). This book addresses how to wean children off of rewards, reasons a student might be cheating, cyberbullying, and other school- and electronics-related topics.

NurtureShock, by Po Bronson and Ashley Merryman (Twelve, 2011). A discussion of recent educational research and its implications, from the critical benefits of sleep to the dangers of incorrect praise.

Your Child's Strengths: A Guide for Parents and Teachers, by Jenifer Fox, MEd (Penguin, 2009). A book that helps parents understand the process and significance of helping children identify how they excel. The checklists in the "My Strengths Inventory" allow students to identify their strengths and find out what these mean about their learning, relationship, and activity styles.

PERIODICALS

Outside of my preferred daily newspaper (the *New York Times*) and assorted weekly news magazines (such as *Time* and the *Week*), here are a few of the publications that I've found most helpful when recommending educational and discussion-worthy articles to students. These are all available in print; many also have original content online and a presence on Facebook and Twitter.

The Atlantic (theatlantic.com). News, culture, technology; ten issues a year.

The American Scholar (theamericanscholar.org). Current events, history, science, culture; quarterly.

The Believer (believermag.com). The arts; ten issues a year.

The Economist (economist.com). World news; weekly.

Fast Company (fastcompany.com). Business, innovation; ten issues a year.

GOOD Magazine (good.is/magazine). "Doing good" culture, commentary, fiction, comics; quarterly.

Harper's Magazine (harpers.org). General interest, culture, *Harper's Index*; monthly.

Lapham's Quarterly (laphamsquarterly.org). Collected historical/modern writing on a theme; quarterly.

National Geographic (ngm.nationalgeographic.com). Geography, science, nature, history, photography; monthly.

New Yorker (newyorker.com). Commentary, nonfiction features, fiction, criticism, cartoons; weekly.

Psychology Today (psychologytoday.com). Human behavior; bimonthly.

Scientific American (scientificamerican.com/sciammag). Science, earth, environment, space; monthly.

Smithsonian (smithsonianmag.com). History, travel, arts, people, places; monthly.

Utne Reader (utne.com/reader). Alternative politics and culture; bimonthly.

READING ALOUD

What to Read When: The Books and Stories to Read with Your Child— and All the Best Times to Read Them, by Pam Allyn (Avery Trade, 2009). How and why to read to children, with themed lists ("Courage," "Loving Numbers," "Sleepovers") of books appropriate for up to age ten.

"How to Mark a Book," by Mortimer J. Adler (academics.keene.edu/ tmendham/documents/AdlerMortimerHowToMarkABook_20060802 .pdf). This 1941 article from the *Saturday Review of Literature* explains how to note important points in books and other reading materials.

How to Read a Book, by Mortimer J. Adler and Charles Van Doren (Touchstone, 1972). The 1940 classic on how to intelligently read and interpret different genres of literature. Includes a list of Adler's recommended "Great Books."

1001 Children's Books You Must Read Before You Grow Up, by Julia Eccleshare (Universe, 2009). A 960-page manual to the best books for children (teens included), divided into five age groupings.

Classics to Read Aloud to Your Children: Selections from Shakespeare, Twain, Dickens, O. Henry, London, Longfellow, Irving, Aesop, Homer, Cervantes, Hawthorne, and More, by William F. Russell (Three Rivers, 1992) and *Classic Myths to Read Aloud: The Great Stories of Greek and Roman Mythology, Specially Arranged for Children Five and Up by an Educational Expert,* by William F. Russell (Broadway, 1992). Both books intended for children from ages five to twelve. Each story includes an "About the Story," an approximate reading time, and vocabulary and pronunciation guide.

The Read-Aloud Handbook, by Jim Trelease (Penguin, 2006). Highly recommended. This book will have you reading (it) aloud within a few pages. It should be required reading for all parents, parents-to-be, grandparents, tutors, and teachers.

100 Best Books for Children: A Parent's Guide to Making the Right Choices for Your Young Reader, Toddler to Preteen, by Anita Silvey (Mariner, 2005). Detailed descriptions of one hundred recommended books, grouped by recommended reading age.

"A Father-Daughter Bond, Page by Page," by Michael Winerip (nytimes.com/2010/03/21/fashion/21GenB.html). Winerip's March 2010 article in the *New York Times* describes the reading ritual that a father and daughter kept up for 3,218 nights, from fourth grade until the start of college.

SCHOOL SUPPLIES

Rainbow Resource Center (rainbowresource.com). Homeschooling books and supplies.

Really Good Stuff (reallygoodstuff.com). Teaching supplies, including the desk privacy screen.

The Pencil Grip (thepencilgrip.com). Pencil grips, sharpeners, and other school supplies.

Magnetic Poetry, Inc. (magneticpoetry.com). Foreign-language magnets, among other refrigerator-friendly options.

SERVICE LEARNING

The Complete Guide to Service Learning: Proven, Practical Ways to Engage Students in Civic Responsibility, Academic Curriculum, & Social Action, by Cathryn Berger Kaye (Free Spirit, 2010). From gardening to AIDS education, this book provides a guide to service learning and, of particular note, literary recommendations that partner well with each category of opportunity.

TECHNOLOGY

Children's Technology Review (childrenstech.com). This monthly print and PDF publication reviews technology products for children up to age fifteen.

Open Culture (openculture.com). This site centralizes links to free resources online, including audiobooks, language lessons, e-books, podcasts, free movies, YouTube channels, and universities that offer free online courses.

Teaching Textbooks (teachingtextbooks.com). This resource offers computer-based courses for individual students.

Notes

CHAPTER 1

1. Taylor, Janna. In conversation with the author. July 2010.

2. Fishbane, Raina. In conversation with the author. August 2010.

CHAPTER 2

1. Brown, Edward Espe. *The Tassajara Bread Book* (Boston: Shambhala, 2009), 111–12.

2. "Resident Life at Georgetown Prep," http://claver.gprep.org/residentlife/.

3. "Children and Sleep," National Sleep Foundation. http://www.sleepfoundation.org/article/sleep-topics/children-and-sleep; "Sleep and Teens," 4. National Sleep Foundation. http://www.sleepfoundation.org/article/ask-the-expert/sleep-and-teens.

4. Bronson, Po, and Ashley Merryman. *NurtureShock*. (New York: Twelve, 2009), 29–44.

CHAPTER 3

1. Lamott, Anne. *Bird by Bird*. (New York: Anchor, 1995), 19.

2. McLane, Katie. In conversation with the author. June 2010.

CHAPTER 4

1. Hulcy, Jessica. In conversation with the author. July 2010.

2. Hunt, Jan. *The Unschooling Unmanual.* (Salt Spring Island, British Columbia, Canada: Natural Child Project, 2008), 72–3.

3. "About Imagination Playground," Imagination Playground. http://www.imaginationplayground.org/about/.

4. Matsumoto, Ryoko. In conversation with the author. April 2010.

5. Charny, Anne. In conversation with the author. May 2010.

CHAPTER 5

1. Gilbreth, Frank, and Gilbreth Carey, Ernestine. *Cheaper by the Dozen.* (New York: HarperCollins, 2005), 24.

2. Ibid., 109.

CHAPTER 6

1. The Henry J. Kaiser Family Foundation, "Generation M^2: Media in the Lives of 8- to 18-Year-Olds" (January 2010). http://www.kff.org/entmedia/upload/8010.pdf.

2. Sandel, Michael. "Justice" (lecture, Harvard University, Cambridge, MA). http://www.justiceharvard.org/index .php?option=com_content&view=article&id=64:discussion-guide-advanced&catid=33:episode-one&Itemid=46

3. U.S. Naval Observatory tour guide. Personal communication. June 28, 2010.

4. American Academy of Pediatrics, Policy Statement on "Children, Adolescents, and Television," *Pediatrics* 107, no. 2 (February 2001): 423–26. http://aappolicy.aappublications. org/cgi/content/full/pediatrics;107/2/423.

5. "Russell Poldrack: Multi-Tasking Adversely Affects the Brain's Learning Systems," University of California, Los Angeles, (July 25, 2006). http://www.psych.ucla.edu/news/russell-poldrack-multi-tasking-adversely-affects-the-brains-learning-systems.

6. Shellenbarger, Sue. "New Studies Show Pitfalls of Doing Too Much at Once," *Wall Street Journal* (February 27, 2003). http://online.wsj.com/article_email/SB1046286576946413103.html.

CHAPTER 7

1. White, Sara. In conversation with the author. July 2010.

2. Oliver, Mary. *A Poetry Handbook*. (Orlando, FL: Harcourt, 1994), 13.

3. McLane, Katie. In conversation with the author. June 2010.

4. Bronson, Po, and Ashley Merryman. *NurtureShock*. (New York: Twelve, 2009), 11–26.

5. Wallace-Segall, Rebecca. In conversation with the author. July 2010.

6. National Tutoring Association, "Tutor Code of Ethics" (2003). http://www.ntatutor.com/code_of_ethics.htm.

CHAPTER 8

1. Trelease, Jim. *The Read-Aloud Handbook*. (New York: Penguin, 2006), 36.

2. Adler, Mortimer J. "How to Mark a Book." *The Saturday Review of Literature* (July 6, 1941). academics.keene.edu/tmendham/documents/AdlerMortimerHowToMarkABook_20060802.pdf

3. Clark, Ron. *The Essential 55: An Award-Winning Educator's Rules for Discovering the Successful Student in Every Child*. (New York: Hyperion, 2003), x.

About the Author

ADAM RUBEN

MARINA KOESTLER RUBEN is a professional tutor, writer, and editor who works as the official in-house writing tutor at the renowned Sidwell Friends School in Washington, DC. She has also privately tutored students (K–12) in math, science, history, English, ESL, French, and Spanish, as well as in organization and study skills. Her former students include public school students, resettled refugees, clients at Potomac Tutors, and high school students at the Melvin J. Berman Hebrew Academy and the Washington International School.

Marina has been published by the *Washington City Paper*, CNN .com, Smithsonian.com, EducationWeek.org, McSweeneys.net, and the Kennedy Center for the Performing Arts, and she has appeared on NPR's *Talk of the Nation*. She has taught children's creative writing workshops for Writopia Lab and adult freelance writing workshops at book festivals.

Marina received her BA and MA from the Johns Hopkins University, where she received the 2008 Outstanding Graduate Award. She lives in Washington, DC, with her husband, Adam, and their recently born tutoring project.

Learn more about her at www.MarinaRuben.com.

Index

C

Calculators, 112
Calendars, 135, 148
Calm, exuding, 46–49
Cameras, digital, 115–16
Canvas or easel, 98
Carle, Eric, 159–60
Catcher in the Rye, The, 63–64, 146
Cell phones
    communication etiquette, 174–75
    smartphone, 113–14, 117
    turning off while tutoring, 21–22
Chalkboard paint, 97–98
Charny, Anne, 89–90
Cheaper by the Dozen, 92–93, 180–81
Cheating, 146–47
Checklists, 168–72
Cheever, John, 32, 33
Children's Technology Review, 111, 187
Clark, Ron, 175, 180
Classes online, 114–15
CliffsNotes, 146
Clocks, 19
Clustering or chunking information, 85
Clutter, 12–13, 14
College student, as tutor, 178
Communication-friendly activities,
    163–64
Computer
    file organization, 130
    games, 119
    labeling files, 132
    microphone for, 123
    saving and storing assignments,
        130–31
    sleep affected by, 39
    use during study time, 37
Consistency, 38
Conversation etiquette, 174–75
"Cosmic Cuisine," 82
Crayons, bath time, 100
Creative tutoring
    boredom and, 89–90
    food for, 80–82
    at-home immersion, 82–83
    importance of, 70–72

    inspirational sources, 72–77
    mnemonics, 25, 84–88
    overview, 91
    playful activities for, 76–80
    silence, using, 88–89
    simplicity, 90
    See also Parent-tutors; Tutoring
Criticism, 53, 152–53
Cuisenaire Rods and base 10 blocks, 18

D

Daily journal, 107
Day planner, 130
Deadlines, handling, 147–48
Desk privacy shield, 37
DiCamillo, Kate, 159–60
Diet. *See* Food
Digital cameras, 115–16
Digital video recorders (DVRs), 116
Dining room, 95–96
Directive tutoring, 11–12
Distractions
    academic, 35
    auditory, 36
    boarding schools restricting, 33–34
    emotional, 36–37
    enhancing child's focus and, 37–38
    famous writers' methods for avoiding,
        32–33
    food needs, 40–42
    inadequate sleep, 38–39
    multitasking, 126–28
    physical well-being issues, 35–36
    recognizing and removing, 34
    social, 36
    technological, 34–35
Doing work for your child, 140–41, 155
Dolls, Waldorf, 73
Drinks, 41–42
Dumbing Us Down, 76, 181
DVRs (digital video recorders), 116

E

Earplugs, 37
eBay, 116
E-books and e-readers, 116–17

tracking, 150
when child is not capable of getting good grades, 157–58
Great Gatsby, The, 53
Greeting your student, 22–23
Grocery lists, magnetic, 95
Guevara, Che, 93

H

Hands-on principle, 75
Helicopter parents, 52, 147–50
Henrichon, Niko, 57
Historical blind spots, 57
History of Private Life, A, 64
History of US, The, 67
Hobart Shakespeareans, The, 60, 180
Holt, John, 73
Home Education Magazine, 82
Home makeover
    bathroom, 99–101
    bedroom, 97–99
    dining room, 95–96
    inside and outside, 101–3
    kitchen, 94–95
    living room, 96–97
    overview, 93–94, 109
    what your house says about you, 103–8
Homeschooling, 73–75, 181–83
Homework. *See* Assignments
Homework notebook or day planner, 130, 147
How to Read a Book, 167
Hugo, Victor, 32, 33
Hulcy, Jessica, 75, 182
Hunt, Jan, 76, 90, 183

I

Imagination Playgrounds, 77
Imitation, plagiarism versus, 143–44
Inspiration (software), 133
Interactive visual aids, 11
Internet
    disabling, 36
    evaluating research sources, 144–45
    online courses and resources, 177
    overreliance on, 136–37

plagiarizing, 142–43
Voice over Internet Protocol (VoIP) devices, 123–24

J

Jefferson, Thomas, 101
Johnny Tremain, 67
Journals, personal, 106–8
Judgment, 54, 58

K

Kitchen, 94–95
Knowledge
    avoiding assumptions about, 54–55
    knowing too little or too much, 10–11
    when you don't know, 29–32
KONOS homeschooling, 75, 182
Koontz, Suzy, 80

L

Labeling/labels, 101, 132
Lamott, Anne, 51–52
Landau, Barry H., 81
Language, 100, 112
Lapbooking, 74
Lap desk, 16
Last Lecture, The, 98, 156
Learning
    focusing on, 157–58
    playful activities for, 76–80
    styles of, 78
    supporting and valuing, 46, 108
    transferring ownership to your child, 11–13
Library, 104–6
Lightning Thief, The, 9
Lincoln, Abraham, 14, 20, 93
Lists
    checklists, 168–72
    grocery, 95
    synonym and thesauri, 22
Living room, 96–97
Love of learning, 13, 44–46

M

Magnets, 94–95
Manipulatives, 18
Map or atlas, 19